Philip's
CHILDREN'S ATLAS

David and Jill Wright

GEORGE PHILIP

CONTENTS

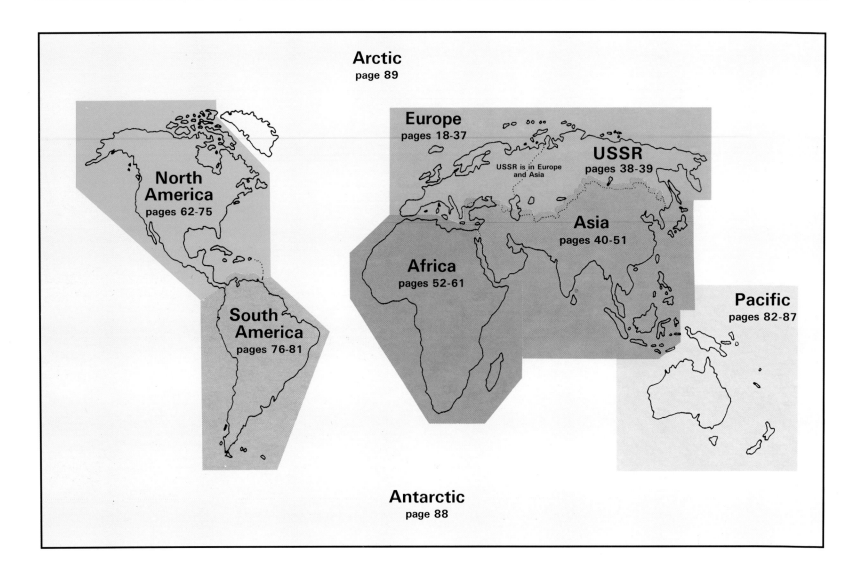

Arctic
page 89

Europe
pages 18-37

USSR
pages 38-39

USSR is in Europe
and Asia

North
America
pages 62-75

Asia
pages 40-51

Africa
pages 52-61

Pacific
pages 82-87

South
America
pages 76-81

Antarctic
page 88

To Rachel and Steven

British Library Cataloguing in Publication Data

Wright, David, 1939–
Philip's children's atlas - 3rd ed.
1. World. Atlases. For children
I. Title   II. Wright, Jill, 1942–
912
ISBN 0-540-05628-6

Text copyright © 1991 by David and Jill Wright
Maps copyright © 1991 George Philip Ltd

First edition 1987
Second edition 1989
Third and revised edition 1991

Printed in Hong Kong

Cover Photographs

Front Cover
Berber Girl, Morocco
Bruno Barbey/Magnum

Back Cover
Market Day in Bida *(see page 56)*
The J. Allan Cash Photolibrary
Wind-pumps in the Netherlands
*(see page 25) The J. Allan Cash
Photolibrary*

4–5 Our Planet Earth

6–7 Mountains, Plains and Seas

8–9 Countries of the World

10–11 People of the World

12–13 Hot and Cold Lands

14–15 Wet and Dry Lands

16–17 Enjoying Maps

18–19 **Europe**
20–21 British Isles
22–23 Scandinavia
24–25 Benelux
26–27 France
28–29 Germany and Austria
30–31 Spain and Portugal
32–33 Switzerland and Italy
34–35 Southeast Europe
36–37 East Europe
38–39 USSR (Europe and Asia)

40–41 **Asia**
42–43 Middle East
44–45 South Asia
46–47 Southeast Asia
48–49 China and Neighbours
50–51 Japan

52–53 **Africa**
54–55 North Africa
56–57 West Africa
58–59 East and Central Africa
60–61 Southern Africa

62–63 **North America**
64–65 Canada
66–67 USA
68–69 Eastern USA
70–71 Western USA
72–73 Central America
74–75 West Indies

76–77 **South America**
78–79 Tropical South America
80–81 Temperate South America

82–83 **The Pacific**
84–85 Australia
86–87 New Zealand

88 Antarctic
89 Arctic

90 Quiz
91 Things To Do
92–95 Index
96 Answers to Questions

OUR PLANET EARTH

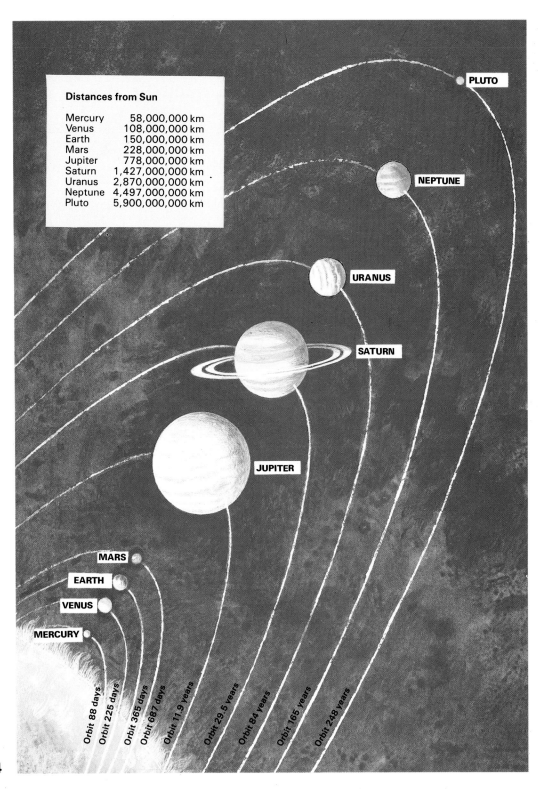

Distances from Sun

Mercury	58,000,000 km
Venus	108,000,000 km
Earth	150,000,000 km
Mars	228,000,000 km
Jupiter	778,000,000 km
Saturn	1,427,000,000 km
Uranus	2,870,000,000 km
Neptune	4,497,000,000 km
Pluto	5,900,000,000 km

PLUTO

NEPTUNE

URANUS

SATURN

JUPITER

MARS

EARTH

VENUS

MERCURY

Orbit 88 days · Orbit 225 days · Orbit 365 days · Orbit 687 days · Orbit 11.9 years · Orbit 29.5 years · Orbit 84 years · Orbit 165 years · Orbit 248 years

Our planet Earth is one of nine planets that travel round the Sun. The diagram (*left*) shows that we are 150 million kilometres away from the Sun. It takes $365\frac{1}{4}$ days for the Earth to travel all the way round the Sun – which we call a year. Every four years we add an extra day to February to use up the $\frac{1}{4}$ days. This is called a Leap Year. The Earth travels at a speed of more than 107,000 kilometres an hour. (In fact, you have travelled 600 kilometres through space while reading this far!)

As the Earth travels through space, it is also spinning round and round. It spins round once in 24 hours, which we call a day. Places on the Equator are spinning at 1660 kilometres an hour. Because of the way the Earth spins, we experience day and night, and different seasons during a year (see page 13). No part of our planet is too hot or too cold for life to survive.

Our nearest neighbour in space is the Moon – 384,400 kilometres away. The first men to reach the Moon took four days to travel there in 1969. On the way, they took photographs of the Earth, such as the one on the right. The Earth looks very blue from space because of all the sea. It is the only planet in the Solar System with sea. Look at the swirls of cloud, especially over southern Africa and over northern Europe. These show that the Earth has an atmosphere. Our atmosphere contains oxygen and water vapour and it keeps us and all other living things alive. We could not breathe on any other planet.

Fact box: Earth

Distance around the Equator
40,075 kilometres

Distance around the poles
40,007 kilometres

Distance to the centre of the Earth 6370 kilometres

Surface area of the Earth
510,065,600 square kilometres
(71% sea; 29% land)

Distance from the Earth to the Sun 150,000,000 kilometres
(It takes $8\frac{1}{2}$ minutes for the Sun's light to reach the Earth.)

Distance from the Earth to the Moon 384,400 kilometres

The Earth travels round the Sun at 107,000 kilometres per hour, or 29.8 kilometres per second

The Earth's atmosphere is about 175 kilometres thick

The chief gases in the atmosphere are nitrogen (78%) and oxygen (21%)

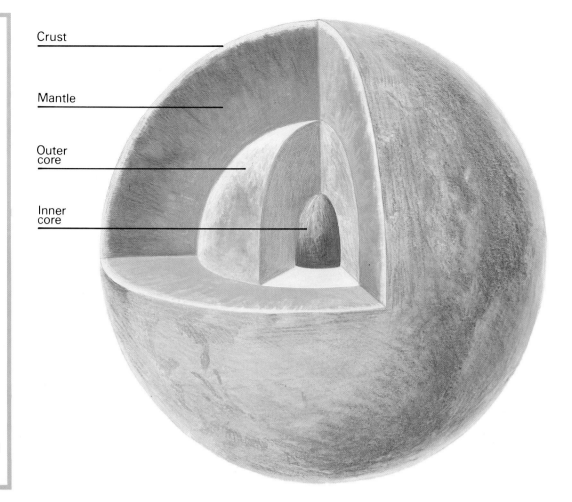

Crust

Mantle

Outer core

Inner core

Scientists believe that our Earth is made of layers of rock. The diagram above shows the Earth with a slice cut out. The hottest part is the core, at the centre. Around the core is the mantle. The outer layer, the crust, is very thin under the oceans, but it is thicker under the continents. Scientists now know that the Earth's crust is cracked, like the shell of a hard-boiled egg that has been dropped. The cracks are called faults. The huge sections of crust divided by the faults are called plates and they are moving very, very slowly. Over millions and millions of years, the continents have gradually moved across the Earth's surface as the crustal plates have moved. Sudden movements near the faults cause earthquakes or volcanic eruptions. The satellite photo (*left*) shows all of Africa and a small part of South America. These two continents were once joined together, but about 100 million years ago they began to split apart.

MOUNTAINS, PLAINS AND SEAS

The map shows that there is much more sea than land in the world. The Pacific is by far the biggest ocean; the map splits it in two.

Mountains are shown in relief on this map. Look for the world's highest mountain range – the Himalayas, in Asia. There are high mountains on the western side of both American continents. Most of the world's great mountain ranges have been made by folding in the Earth's crust.

Desert areas are in orange. The green expanse across northern Europe and northern Asia is the world's biggest plain.

Part of the Great Plains of North America. *The land is flat as far as the eye can see, but it is also 1000 metres above sea-level – plains are not always lowland.*

▽

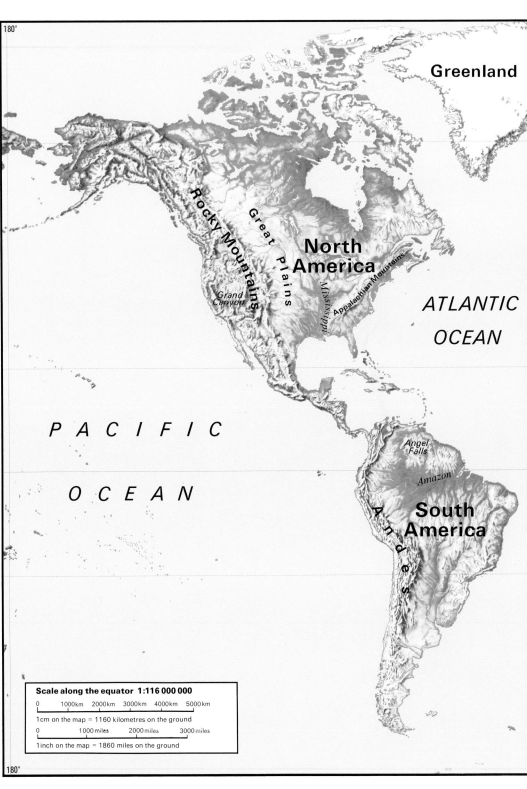

180°

Greenland

Rocky Mountains

Great Plains

North America

Grand Canyon

Mississippi

Appalachian Mountains

ATLANTIC OCEAN

P A C I F I C

O C E A N

Angel Falls

Amazon

Andes

South America

Scale along the equator 1:116 000 000

| 0 | 1000km | 2000km | 3000km | 4000km | 5000km |

1cm on the map = 1160 kilometres on the ground

| 0 | 1000 miles | 2000 miles | 3000 miles |

1inch on the map = 1860 miles on the ground

180°

Fact box

Highest mountain Mount Everest, 8848 metres (Asia)

Longest mountain range Andes, 7200 kilometres (S. America)

Longest rivers Nile, 6670 kilometres (Africa); Amazon, 6448 kilometres (S. America)

Longest gorge Grand Canyon, 349 kilometres (N. America)

Highest waterfall Angel Falls, 979 metres (Venezuela, S. America)

Largest lake Caspian Sea, 360,700 square kilometres (USSR and Iran, Asia)

Deepest lake Lake Baikal, 1940 metres (USSR)

Largest ocean Pacific, 181,000,000 square kilometres

Deepest part of oceans Mariana Trench, 10,924 metres (Pacific)

Largest islands Australia, 7,686,848 square kilometres; Greenland, 2,175,600 square kilometres

Largest desert Sahara, 8,400,000 square kilometres (Africa)

COUNTRIES OF THE WORLD

Five of the continents of the world are divided into countries. Most countries are now independent and manage their own affairs. A few of the smaller countries and islands are still ruled by another country.

Look at the boundaries between countries. Some follow natural features, such as rivers or mountain ranges. Straight boundaries were drawn for convenience. Often they separate people of the same language or tribe, and this can create problems.

The United Nations building, *in New York, USA. The world's problems are discussed here – and sometimes solved. Almost every country has a representative at the United Nations.*

B. = BHUTAN
BUR. = BURUNDI
BEL. = BELGIUM
L. = LEBANON
LUX. = LUXEMBOURG
N. = NETHERLANDS
R. = RWANDA
S. = SWITZERLAND
U.A.E. = UNITED ARAB EMIRATES

Scale along the equator 1:116 000 000

| 0 | 1000km | 2000km | 3000km | 4000km | 5000km |

1cm on the map = 1160 kilometres on the ground

| 0 | 1000miles | 2000miles | 3000miles |

1inch on the map = 1860miles on the ground

Fact box

Only five of the 'top ten' countries with large populations are also among the 'top ten' biggest countries. Check which they are. Asia has 6½* of the ten most populated countries – but only 2½* of the 'top ten' biggest countries. *USSR is in both Asia and Europe.

Top ten countries by size (square kilometres)

1 USSR	22,402,200	6 Australia	7,686,848
2 Canada	9,976,140	7 India	3,287,590
3 China	9,597,000	8 Argentina	2,776,889
4 USA	9,363,123	9 Sudan	2,505,813
5 Brazil	8,511,965	10 Algeria	2,381,741

Top ten countries by population (UN figures)

1 China	1,134 million	6 Brazil	151 million
2 India	854 million	7 Japan	124 million
3 USSR	291 million	8 Nigeria	119 million
4 USA	252 million	9 Bangladesh	115 million
5 Indonesia	190 million	10 Pakistan	115 million

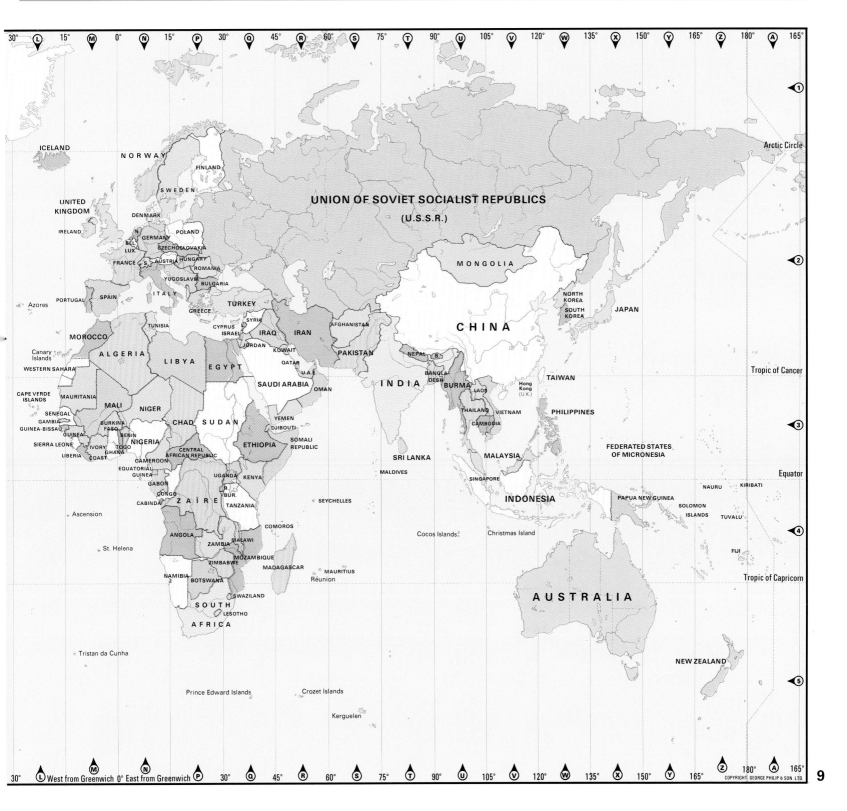

PEOPLE OF THE WORLD

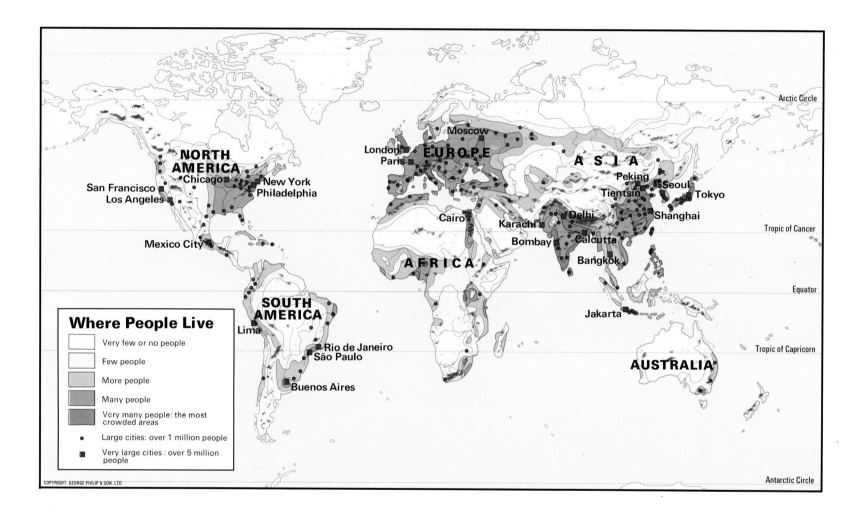

Where People Live

- Very few or no people
- Few people
- More people
- Many people
- Very many people: the most crowded areas
- • Large cities: over 1 million people
- ■ Very large cities : over 5 million people

COPYRIGHT. GEORGE PHILIP & SON. LTD

There is *one* race of people: the human race. In Latin, we are all known as *Homo sapiens* – 'wise person'. The differences between people, such as dark or light skin, hair and eyes, are quite small.

But the differences in wealth are enormous. In any one country there are rich and poor people; but the differences between countries are even greater. The poorest countries are in the Tropics – especially in Africa (south of the Sahara) and south Asia. People are about fifty times richer in some countries of the Middle East and northwest Europe, Japan, the USA and Canada. These are the world's richest countries.

Watering onions in the Gambia, West Africa. *This boy's watering-can was given by the 'Freedom from Hunger Campaign', to help the family grow more food. Many schemes like this are helped by money from people in the rich countries of the world.*

The main map (*opposite*) shows where the world's people live. Most of the world has very few people: notice that large areas are shown in yellow. Compare these areas with the maps on pages 6–7 and 14–15 and you will see that they are mostly desert, or high mountains, or densely forested, or very cold. So some remaining areas, where crops grow well, are very crowded indeed. Over half the world's people live in the lowlands of south and east Asia. Other crowded areas are parts of northwest Europe, the Nile valley and northeast USA. The most crowded places of all are the big cities.

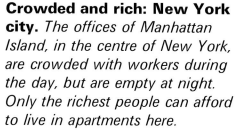

The Developed World

The Developing World
(The Third World)

Rich Countries				Poor Countries		
The very rich	The rich	Just above-average-	▲	Just below	The poor	The very poor

Empty and poor: nomads in the **Sahara.** *Bedouin nomads drink a cup of tea in the Sahara desert. They may be poor, but they are ready to welcome and help other travellers. The world's deserts are empty except where crops can be irrigated – as in the Nile valley.*

Crowded and poor: shanty town in Brazil. *These shanties on a steep hillside in Rio de Janeiro were built by people who have nowhere else to live. Poverty in the countryside forces people to the cities, but it is hard to find a job if you have no skills.*

The smaller map (*above*) shows the richer parts of the world where people usually get enough to eat, and the poorer parts where they are often hungry. Some of the poorest people live in shanty towns (see below).

Crowded and rich: New York city. *The offices of Manhattan Island, in the centre of New York, are crowded with workers during the day, but are empty at night. Only the richest people can afford to live in apartments here.*
▽

HOT AND COLD LANDS

Five important lines are drawn across these maps of the world: the Arctic and Antarctic Circles; the Tropics of Cancer and Capricorn; and the Equator. They divide the world roughly into the *polar*, *temperate* and *tropical* zones.

◁ **Arctic winter.** *Winter begins early in Greenland. These fishing boats are frozen in the harbour at Angmagssalik. From late September the days get shorter, until there are 24 hours of dark and cold at Christmas-time.*

The *polar* lands remain cold all through the year, even though the summer days are so long that the snow can melt.

The *tropical* lands are always hot, except where mountains or plateaus reach high above sea-level. For some of the year the Sun is directly overhead.

The *temperate* lands have four seasons: summer and winter, with spring and autumn in between. But these seasons come at different times of the year north and south of the Equator.

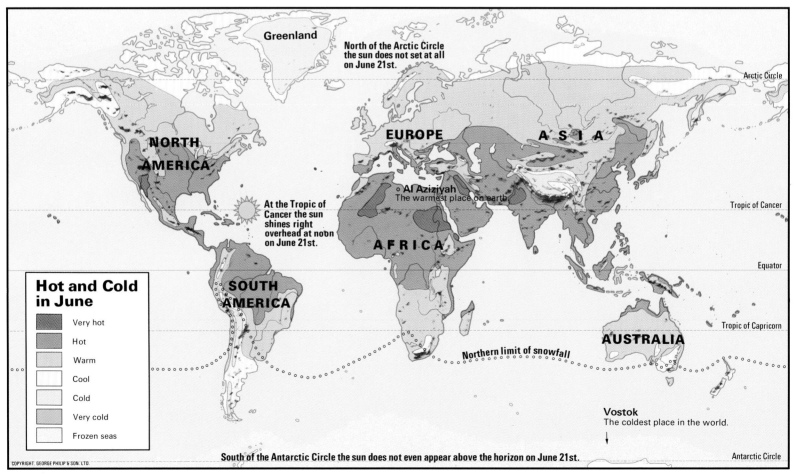

Greenland

North of the Arctic Circle the sun does not set at all on June 21st.

Arctic Circle

NORTH AMERICA

EUROPE

ASIA

At the Tropic of Cancer the sun shines right overhead at noon on June 21st.

Al Aziziyah
The warmest place on earth

Tropic of Cancer

AFRICA

Equator

Hot and Cold in June

	Very hot
	Hot
	Warm
	Cool
	Cold
	Very cold
	Frozen seas

SOUTH AMERICA

Tropic of Capricorn

AUSTRALIA

Northern limit of snowfall

Vostok
The coldest place in the world.

South of the Antarctic Circle the sun does not even appear above the horizon on June 21st.

Antarctic Circle

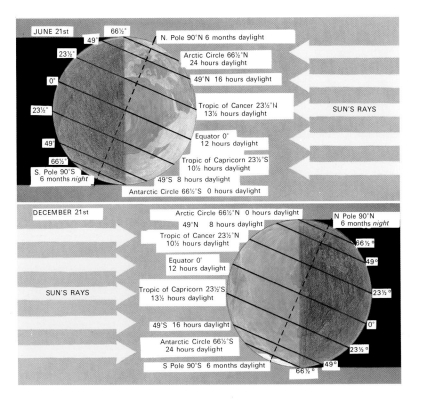

JUNE 21st

66½°
49°
23½°
0°
23½°
49°
66½°

N. Pole 90°N 6 months daylight
Arctic Circle 66½°N 24 hours daylight
49°N 16 hours daylight
Tropic of Cancer 23½°N 13½ hours daylight
Equator 0° 12 hours daylight
Tropic of Capricorn 23½°S 10½ hours daylight
49°S 8 hours daylight
Antarctic Circle 66½°S 0 hours daylight
S. Pole 90°S 6 months *night*

SUN'S RAYS

DECEMBER 21st

Arctic Circle 66½°N 0 hours daylight
49°N 8 hours daylight
Tropic of Cancer 23½°N 10½ hours daylight
Equator 0° 12 hours daylight
Tropic of Capricorn 23½°S 13½ hours daylight
49°S 16 hours daylight
Antarctic Circle 66½°S 24 hours daylight
S Pole 90°S 6 months daylight

N Pole 90°N 6 months *night*
66½°
49°
23½°
0°
23½°
66½°
49°

SUN'S RAYS

Fact box

Hottest recorded temperature 58°C at Al Aziziyah in Libya

Coldest recorded temperature −89.2°C at Vostok in Antarctica

Greatest change of temperature at one place in a year From −70°C to +36.7°C at Verkhoyansk in Siberia, USSR

Highest rainfall in 1 month and in 1 year 9299 mm in 1 month and 26,461 mm in 1 year at Cherrapunji, India (see map page 14)

Most rainy days 350 days in a year at Mount Wai-'ale-'ale in Hawaii (see map page 14)

Wettest place on average Over 1 metre of rain a year at Tutunendo in Colombia (see map page 14)

Driest place In the Atacama desert, northern Chile, with *no* rain for 400 years! (See map page 14)

Most thunder 322 days in a year with thunder at Bogor in Java, Indonesia

The diagrams above help to explain why the seasons vary north and south of the Equator. In June (*top*) the Sun is overhead at the Tropic of Cancer. The North Pole is tilted towards the Sun, and the Arctic enjoys 24 hours of daylight. It is summer in North America, Europe and Asia. Notice that Antarctica is in total darkness.

By December, the Earth has travelled half-way round the Sun. Spot the difference in December (*below*). Where is the Sun overhead? Now Antarctica has 24 hours of daylight. It is summer in the southern continents, so children in Australia open Christmas presents in their summer holidays (see page 85).

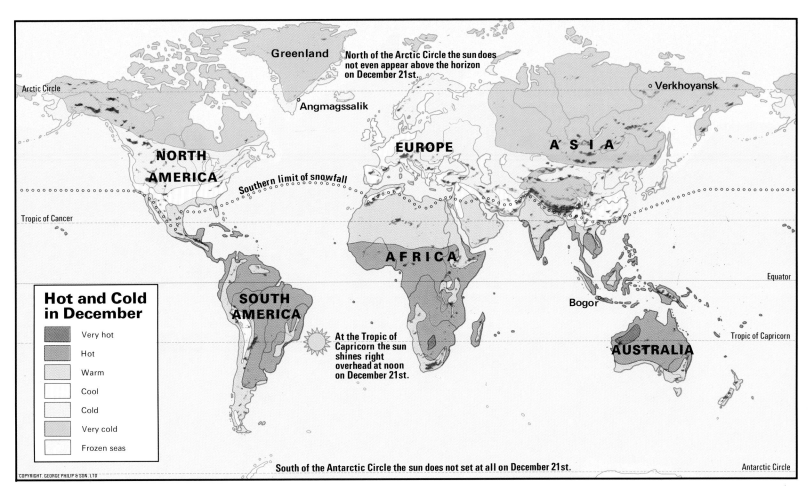

North of the Arctic Circle the sun does not even appear above the horizon on December 21st.

Greenland

Arctic Circle

Verkhoyansk

Angmagssalik

NORTH AMERICA

EUROPE

ASIA

Southern limit of snowfall

Tropic of Cancer

AFRICA

At the Tropic of Capricorn the sun shines right overhead at noon on December 21st.

SOUTH AMERICA

Bogor

Equator

Tropic of Capricorn

AUSTRALIA

Hot and Cold in December

- Very hot
- Hot
- Warm
- Cool
- Cold
- Very cold
- Frozen seas

South of the Antarctic Circle the sun does not set at all on December 21st.

Antarctic Circle

WET AND DRY LANDS

△ **Burning the savanna,** *in northern Ghana, West Africa. At the end of the long dry season, farmers burn the bush (long grass and small trees). The land will be ready for planting crops as soon as the wet season begins.*

Water is needed by all living things. The map below shows that different parts of the world receive different amounts of water. Follow the Equator: most places near the Equator are very wet as well as being very hot. The map opposite shows that near the Equator there are large areas of thick forest. Here, it rains almost every day. Now follow the Tropic of Cancer and the Tropic of Capricorn on both maps. The Tropics cross areas of desert, where it is dry all year. Between the desert and the forest is an area of tall grass and bushes called the savanna. People here talk about the 'wet' and 'dry' seasons. For part of the year it is as rainy as at the Equator; for the rest of the year it is as dry as the desert.

North of the Sahara desert is the Mediterranean Sea. Places around this sea have lovely hot, dry summers, but they do have rain in winter. There are areas near other deserts with a similar climate, such as California in North America and central Chile in South America.

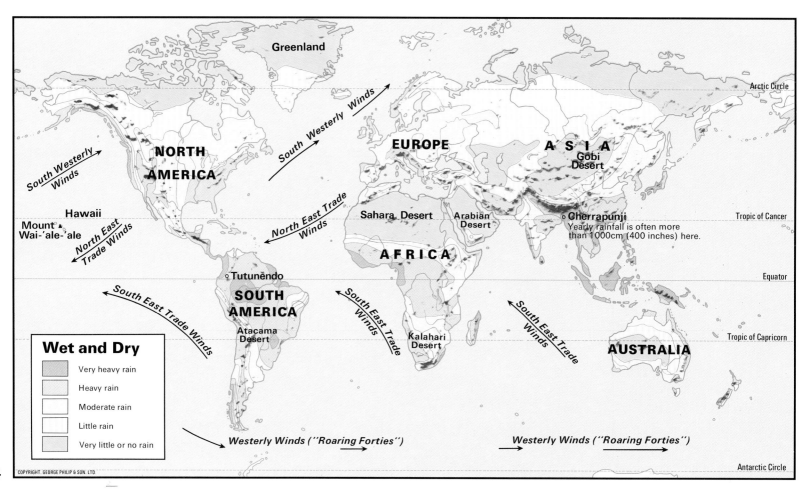

Greenland

Arctic Circle

South Westerly Winds

NORTH AMERICA

EUROPE

ASIA
Gobi Desert

Hawaii

Mount Wai-'ale-'ale

North East Trade Winds

South Westerly Winds

North East Trade Winds

Sahara Desert

Arabian Desert

Cherrapunji
Yearly rainfall is often more than 1000cm (400 inches) here.

Tropic of Cancer

AFRICA

Tutunendo

SOUTH AMERICA

South East Trade Winds

South East Trade Winds

Kalahari Desert

South East Trade Winds

Equator

Atacama Desert

AUSTRALIA

Tropic of Capricorn

Wet and Dry

- Very heavy rain
- Heavy rain
- Moderate rain
- Little rain
- Very little or no rain

Westerly Winds ("Roaring Forties")

Westerly Winds ("Roaring Forties")

Antarctic Circle

14

Forest and mountains in Alberta, Canada. The coniferous trees can survive Canada's bitterly cold winters. In the high mountains, trees cannot grow: it is too cold and the soil is too thin. Similar forests stretch across northern Europe and Asia, in Scandinavia and the USSR. The wood may be used for paper for books.

Desert in Namibia, southern Africa. The Namib Desert has given its name to the country of Namibia. It is a very dry area, west of the Kalahari desert. Winds usually blow away from the land, so rain is very rare.

In the temperate lands, many places have some rain all through the year. Damp winds from the sea bring plenty of rain to the coastal areas, and trees grow well. London and New York have some rain every month. Far inland, near the centre of the continents, and where high mountains cut off the sea winds, it is much drier. Here, there are vast grasslands, like the prairies of North America.

The Arctic and Antarctic lands are nearly as dry as the hot deserts. But the moisture collects as snow. Where the snow melts in the short summer, flowers and small plants grow in the marshy soil – called the tundra.

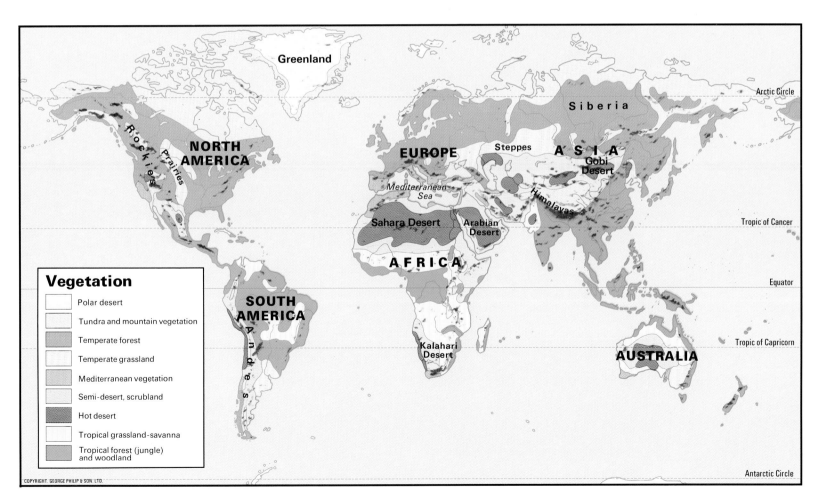

Vegetation

	Polar desert
	Tundra and mountain vegetation
	Temperate forest
	Temperate grassland
	Mediterranean vegetation
	Semi-desert, scrubland
	Hot desert
	Tropical grassland-savanna
	Tropical forest (jungle) and woodland

ENJOYING MAPS

An atlas is a book of maps. The maps in this book have been carefully drawn by cartographers (map-makers) to tell us about the countries of the world.

The maps on pages 6 to 15 show the whole world. Because the world is round, the best model is a globe. It is impossible to draw a really accurate map of the round world on a flat piece of paper. This is why the Pacific Ocean is cut in half, and Antarctica becomes a long thin strip. On pages 88 and 89 there are maps of parts of the world viewed from a different angle.

The maps on pages 18 to 89 show the continents and countries of the world. Each map has a key, with information that will help you 'read' the map. Use your imagination to 'see' what the land is like in each part of the world that you visit through these pages. The photos and text will make your picture clearer.

These two pages explain the key to all the maps. The country of Ghana is used as an example. Ghana is in square

The border between Ghana and Burkina Faso.
The red lines on the map show the boundaries between countries. When travelling from one country to another, you have to stop at the border. These children live in Ghana, and the Ghana flag is flying on their side of the border.

The message on the arch says 'Bye-bye; safe journey'. In Ghana, most officials speak English, and people drive on the left. But in Burkina Faso officials speak French and people drive on the right.

B2 of the map *(right)*. Find 🚩 at the top of the map with one finger, and ➤ at the side of the map with another finger. Move each finger in the direction of the arrows; Ghana is where they meet. The stamps and photograph on this page come from Ghana.

The capital city of each country is underlined on the maps. The rulers of the country live in the capital city, and it is the biggest city in most countries. But not all capital cities are big. On this map, you can see three sizes of city. The biggest ones are marked by a square; they have over one million people. Middle-sized cities have a big dot, and smaller cities have a small dot. Small towns and villages are not shown on maps of this scale, but some have been included in this atlas because they are mentioned in the text.

Countries that are coloured bright yellow on the map are shown in more detail on other pages. The small inset map shows where the main map fits into the continent of Africa. Maps of the whole of Africa are at the beginning of the Africa section (pages 52–3).

This is your chance to explore Africa – enjoy yourself!

Postage stamps

Postage stamps are on many pages of this atlas. You can learn so much from stamps! For example: the map shows you that Ghana is a country; the stamps tell you the official language of Ghana, and show you Ghana's flag.

The map tells you the name of Ghana's biggest lake (man-made). The 6Np stamp shows you the dam and tells you its name.

The map tells you that Ghana has a coastline; the 10Np stamp tells you the name of Ghana's main port, and shows you the big modern cranes there. Np stands for new pesewas (100 pesewas = 1 cedi).

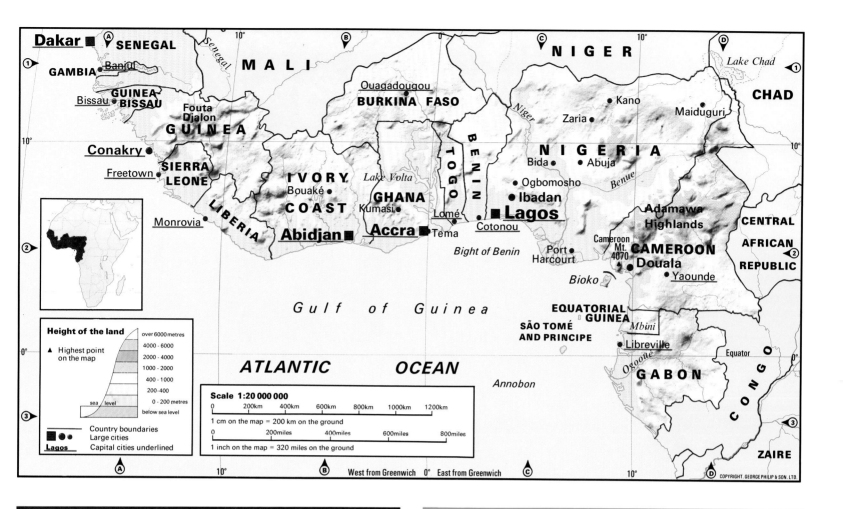

The map includes the following labels:

Dakar ■, SENEGAL, GAMBIA, Banjul, MALI, Senegal, Ouagadougou, BURKINA FASO, NIGER, Lake Chad, CHAD, GUINEA BISSAU, Bissau ●, Fouta Djalon, GUINEA, Kano, Zaria, Maiduguri, Conakry ●, Niger, NIGERIA, SIERRA LEONE, Freetown, Bida, Abuja, Bouaké, IVORY COAST, Lake Volta, GHANA, Ogbomosho, Benue, Adamawa Highlands, CENTRAL AFRICAN REPUBLIC, Kumasi, Ibadan, LIBERIA, Abidjan ■, Accra ■, Lomé, Tema, Lagos, Cotonou, Cameroon Mt. 4070, Monrovia, TOGO, BENIN, Port Harcourt, CAMEROON, Douala, Yaounde, Bight of Benin, Bioko, Gulf of Guinea, EQUATORIAL GUINEA, SÃO TOMÉ AND PRINCIPE, Mbini, Libreville, Equator, GABON, ATLANTIC OCEAN, Annobon, Ogooue, CONGO, ZAIRE

Height of the land

▲ Highest point on the map

over 6000 metres
4000 - 6000
2000 - 4000
1000 - 2000
400 - 1000
200 - 400
sea level 0 - 200 metres
below sea level

Country boundaries
Large cities
Lagos Capital cities underlined

Scale 1:20 000 000

0 | 200km | 400km | 600km | 800km | 1000km | 1200km

1 cm on the map = 200 km on the ground

0 | 200miles | 400miles | 600miles | 800miles

1 inch on the map = 320 miles on the ground

COPYRIGHT. GEORGE PHILIP & SON. LTD.

West from Greenwich 0° East from Greenwich

Scale

Scale 1:20 000 000

0 | 200km | 400km | 600km | 800km | 1000km | 1200km

1 cm on the map = 200 km on the ground

0 | 200miles | 400miles | 600miles | 800miles

1 inch on the map = 320 miles on the ground

This box
shows
the scale
of the map. The scale is written in different ways.
The map is drawn to a scale of 1:20,000,000,
which means that the distance between two
places on the ground is exactly twenty million
times bigger than it is on this page! Other maps
in this atlas are drawn to different scales: little
Belgium (page 24) is drawn at a scale of
1:2 million, while the largest country in the
world is drawn at a scale of 1:45 million (USSR,
page 38). Another way of writing the scale of this
map is to say that 1 centimetre on the map is
equal to 200 kilometres on the ground in West
Africa. And this is how the scale line is drawn.

You can use the scale line to make your own
scale ruler. Put the straight edge of a strip of
paper against the scale line and mark the
position of 200, 400, 600 kilometres, etc. (Or use
the scale in miles if you prefer.) Carefully
number each mark. Now move your scale ruler
over the map to see how far it is between places.
For example, Accra to Abidjan is 400 kilometres.

Height of the land

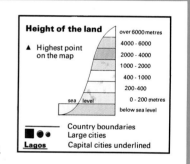

Height of the land

▲ Highest point on the map

over 6000 metres
4000 - 6000
2000 - 4000
1000 - 2000
400 - 1000
200 - 400
sea level 0 - 200 metres
below sea level

Country boundaries
Large cities
Lagos Capital cities underlined

The countries of West
Africa are coloured so
that you can tell the
height of the land. Green
shows the lowest land.
Often the real land will not look green – in the
dry season the grass is brown. The higher land is
coloured yellow or brown, even though some
parts are covered with thick green forest! The
highest point in West Africa is shown with a
small black triangle – find it in square C2 – but
the mountains are not high enough to be shown
in mauve or white: look for these on page 44.
And to find land *below* sea-level, try page 24.
Cameroon has some dramatic mountains (see
page 57), but elsewhere the change from lowland
to highland is often quite gentle.

Water features are shown in blue, and their
names are in *italic print*. These include the sea,
big rivers and lakes, such as *Lake Chad* (D1)
and *Lake Volta* (B2). Blue dashes show rivers
which dry up for some of the year.

EUROPE

The map shows the great North European plain that stretches from the Atlantic Ocean to the USSR. This plain has most of Europe's best farmland, and many of the biggest cities. To the north of the plain are the snowy mountains of Scandinavia. To the south are even higher mountains: the Pyrenees, the Alps and Carpathians, and the Caucasus Mountains of the USSR.

Southern Europe has hills and mountains by the Mediterranean Sea. The small areas of lowland are carefully farmed.

Puzzle picture
Western Europe's most important building.
★What building is it?
★Where is it?
★Why does it look so strange?
(Answers on page 96.)

These twelve car-plates are from the twelve countries of the European Community (Common Market). Can you name them?

(Answers on page 96.)

18

Germany/Austria border. *There are many contrasts in Europe. This photograph shows farmland (foreground); woodland (centre); and mountains (the Alps, in the background); find the Alps on the map on page 18. Another important contrast is not visible. The foreground is in Germany, a big country; the background is in Austria, a small country.*

▼

Fact box: Europe

Area 10,531,000 square kilometres (including European USSR)

Highest point Mt Elbrus (USSR), 5633 metres

Lowest point Shores of Caspian Sea (USSR), 38 metres below sea level

Longest river Volga (USSR), 3690 kilometres

Largest lake Caspian Sea* (USSR), 360,700 square kilometres

Biggest country USSR*, 22,402,200 square kilometres (total area)

Smallest country Vatican City* (in Rome, Italy), less than half a square kilometre

Richest country Switzerland

Poorest country Albania

Most crowded country Malta

Least crowded country Iceland

*A *world record* as well as a European record

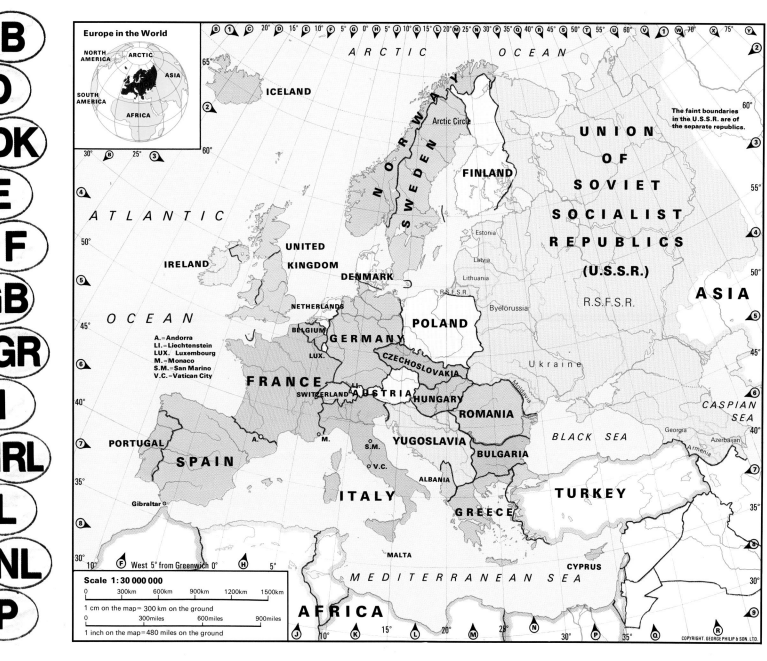

Europe in the World

NORTH AMERICA ARCTIC ASIA AFRICA SOUTH AMERICA

The faint boundaries in the U.S.S.R. are of the separate republics.

A. = Andorra
LI. = Liechtenstein
LUX. Luxembourg
M. = Monaco
S.M. = San Marino
V.C. = Vatican City

Scale 1:30 000 000

| 0 | 300km | 600km | 900km | 1200km | 1500km |

1 cm on the map = 300 km on the ground

| 0 | 300miles | 600miles | 900miles |

1 inch on the map = 480 miles on the ground

COPYRIGHT. GEORGE PHILIP & SON. LTD.

BRITISH ISLES

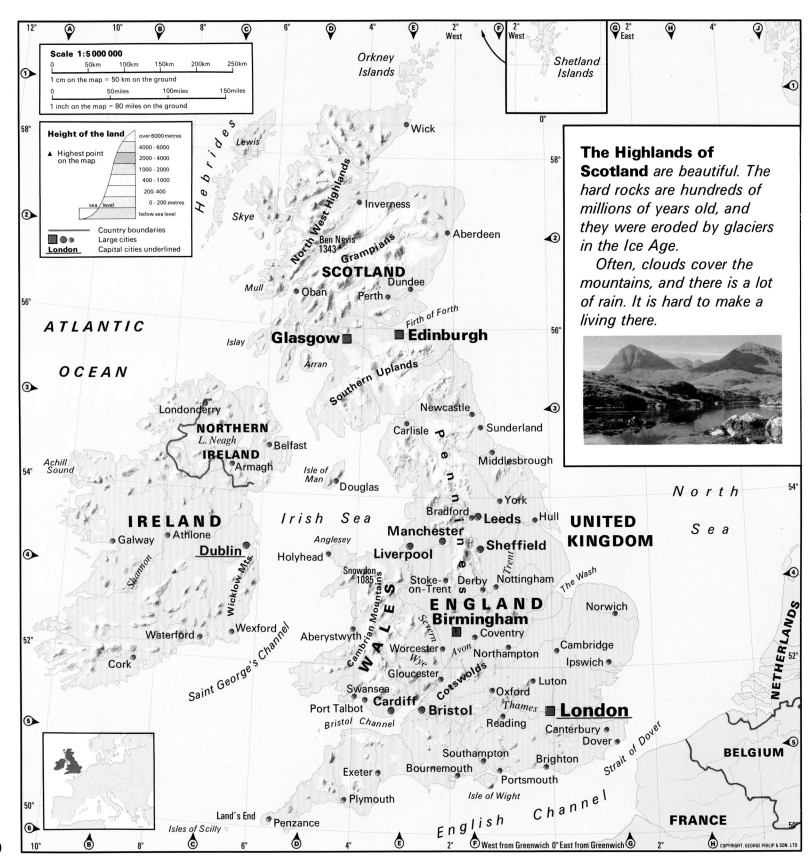

Scale 1:5 000 000

0   50km   100km   150km   200km   250km

1 cm on the map = 50 km on the ground

0   50miles   100miles   150miles

1 inch on the map = 80 miles on the ground

Height of the land

over 6000 metres
4000 - 6000
▲ Highest point on the map
2000 - 4000
1000 - 2000
400 - 1000
200-400
sea level   0 - 200 metres
below sea level

Country boundaries
Large cities
London   Capital cities underlined

The Highlands of Scotland *are beautiful. The hard rocks are hundreds of millions of years old, and they were eroded by glaciers in the Ice Age.*

Often, clouds cover the mountains, and there is a lot of rain. It is hard to make a living there.

Orkney Islands

Shetland Islands

Hebrides

Lewis

Wick

Skye

North West Highlands

Inverness

Ben Nevis 1343

Grampians

Aberdeen

SCOTLAND

Mull

Oban

Perth

Dundee

ATLANTIC

Firth of Forth

Glasgow   **Edinburgh**

Islay

Arran

OCEAN

Southern Uplands

Newcastle

Londonderry

Carlisle

Sunderland

NORTHERN
L. Neagh

Belfast

Middlesbrough

IRELAND

Armagh

Isle of Man

Douglas

P e n n i n e s

Achill Sound

York

North Sea

IRELAND

Irish Sea

Bradford   Leeds   Hull

UNITED

Galway   Athlone

Anglesey

Manchester

Sheffield

KINGDOM

Dublin

Holyhead

Liverpool

Shannon

Snowdon 1085

Stoke-on-Trent

Derby   Nottingham

The Wash

Wicklow Mts.

Cambrian Mountains

Trent

E N G L A N D

Norwich

Waterford   Wexford

Aberystwyth

Birmingham

Coventry

Cambridge

Cork

Worcester   Avon   Northampton

Ipswich

Wye

Gloucester

Cotswolds

Luton

Swansea

Oxford

Saint George's Channel

Port Talbot   **Cardiff**   **Bristol**

Thames

London

Bristol Channel

Reading

Canterbury

Dover

BELGIUM

Southampton   Brighton

Strait of Dover

Exeter   Bournemouth

Portsmouth

Plymouth

Isle of Wight

NETHERLANDS

Land's End   Penzance

English Channel

FRANCE

Isles of Scilly

WALES

Severn

What do the flags mean?

The Union Jack is made up of three flags: the red-on-white cross (+) of St George (England); the white-on-blue cross (×) of St Andrew (Scotland); and the red-on-white cross (×) of St Patrick (Ireland) – although most of Ireland is independent! St David (Wales) is not included, even though Wales is part of the UK.

The Republic of Ireland flag shows a white stripe (for peace) between orange (Protestants) and green (Roman Catholics).

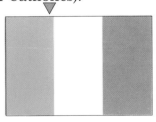

The Cotswolds, England, *are limestone hills. A little village built long ago from the limestone rock nestles at the foot of the hill, where a spring gives pure water. Woodland, grassland and ploughed land still cover much of England.*

The United Kingdom is made up of Great Britain (England, Scotland and Wales) and Northern Ireland. The UK was the most important country in the world 150 years ago. Many old factories and coal-mines have now closed down, and several million people have no jobs. Unemployment is worst in the north. Much of the UK is still quiet and beautiful (see photograph above).

The Republic of Ireland is a completely separate country from the UK. There were twice as many people in Ireland 150 years ago as there are today. In the west, many abandoned

Can you spot eight famous London landmarks on this stamp? (Answer on page 96.)

farms can be seen. Farming is still important, and Irish butter and cream are famous. New factories have been built in many towns.

Industry in South Wales. *This is the BP chemical works at Port Talbot, between Swansea and Cardiff. The big towers are cooling towers. The tall chimney on the right is part of the power station for the site. You can see sand-dunes in the foreground.*

Ireland: harvesting reeds. *In the ▷ far west of Ireland, traditional scenes like this can sometimes still be seen. But tractors are more common nowadays. This view is near Achill Sound.*

SCANDINAVIA

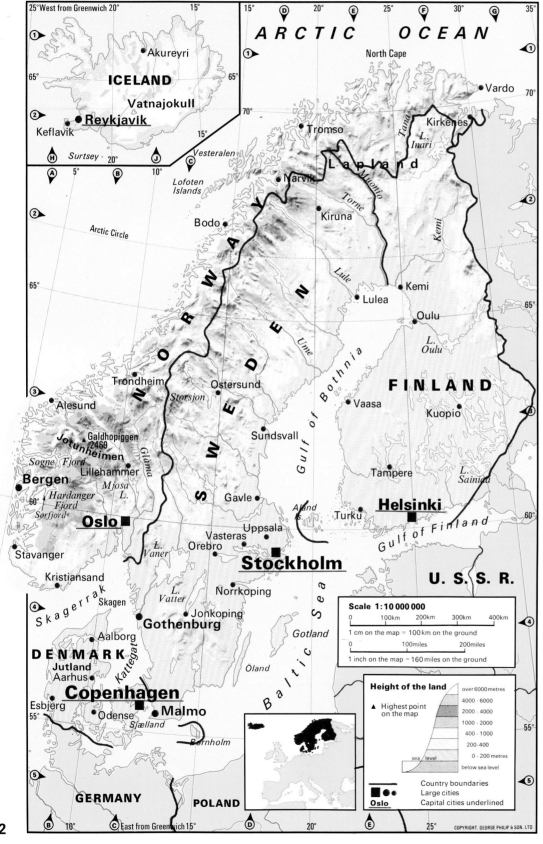

ARCTIC OCEAN

North Cape

Vardo

Akureyri

ICELAND

Vatnajokull

Reykjavik

Keflavik

Surtsey

Vesteralen

Lofoten Islands

Arctic Circle

Tromso

Kirkenes

L. Inari

Tana

Narvik

Lapland

Muonio

Torne

Kiruna

Kemi

Bodo

Lule

Lulea

Kemi

Oulu

L. Oulu

N O R W A Y

S W E D E N

FINLAND

Trondheim

Ostersund

Storsjon

Alesund

Vaasa

Kuopio

Galdhopiggen 2469

Jotunheimen

Glama

Sogne Fjord

Bergen

Lillehammer

Hardanger Fjord

Sørfjord

Mjosa L.

Gulf of Bothnia

Sundsvall

Gavle

Tampere

L. Sainiaa

Oslo

Vasteras

Orebro

Uppsala

Aland Is

Turku

Helsinki

Stavanger

L. Vaner

Gulf of Finland

Kristiansand

L. Vatter

Stockholm

Norrkoping

U. S. S. R.

Skagerrak

Skagen

Jonkoping

Gothenburg

Gotland

Baltic Sea

Aalborg

Kattegat

DENMARK

Jutland

Aarhus

Öland

Copenhagen

Esbjerg

Odense

Sjælland

Malmo

Bornholm

GERMANY

POLAND

Scale 1:10 000 000

| 0 | 100km | 200km | 300km | 400km |

1 cm on the map = 100 km on the ground

| 0 | 100miles | 200miles |

1 inch on the map = 160 miles on the ground

Height of the land

▲ Highest point on the map

over 6000 metres
4000 - 6000
2000 - 4000
1000 - 2000
400 - 1000
200 - 400
sea level   0 - 200 metres
below sea level

■ Country boundaries
■● Large cities
Oslo Capital cities underlined

COPYRIGHT. GEORGE PHILIP & SON. LTD

Land of ice and fire

Iceland has many volcanoes. Most are quiet and peaceful.

▽

EUROPA CEPT

ÍSLAND 85

JARDELDAR Á HEIMAEY 1973

ÍSLAND 25

△

But . . . sometimes a great volcanic eruption lights up the night sky and the light is reflected in the sea.

Only 250,000 people live in **Iceland**. It is near the Arctic Circle and there is ice on the mountains, in glaciers and ice-sheets. The sea stays ice-free and is full of fish. Iceland has an important fishing fleet.

△

Sørfjord *is a branch of Hardanger Fjord on the west coast of Norway. A fjord is a long, narrow, deep inlet of the sea with steep sides. Fjords were dug by valley glaciers in the Ice Age. Here the sides are so steep that the road is cut in solid rock. The cars show how steep and high the fjord sides are.*

22

Forests and lakes in Finland.
Most of southern Finland is forested. The ice-sheets scraped hollows in the rocks and there are lots of beautiful lakes. The trees are cut down for timber, woodpulp, paper, chipboard, matches and other products that are sold abroad.

The mountains of Norway and Iceland are high and rugged. There are ice-sheets and glaciers even today. You can see snow on the highest land in the photograph of the fjord.

Southern Sweden and all of Denmark are lowland. This land was formed from sand and gravel brought by ice-sheets in the Ice Age. The sandy parts do not have good soil, but

the clay lands grow very good crops.

The five countries of Scandinavia have small populations. Most people live in towns and cities, and hardly anyone is poor. There are very few people in Lapland in the far north, which lies inside the Arctic Circle.

Reindeer in Lapland. *Lapland is the northern part of Norway, Sweden and Finland, where the Lapps live. They keep reindeer for their milk, meat and leather, and to pull sledges. Notice the warm and colourful clothes the Lapps wear.*

Gothenburg *is the main port on* ▷ *the west coast of Sweden. The sea does not freeze here for long.*

Legoland *is a model village beside the Lego factory in Denmark. Everything is made of Lego! This is a model of a fishing village in the Lofoten Islands of Norway.*
▽

BENELUX

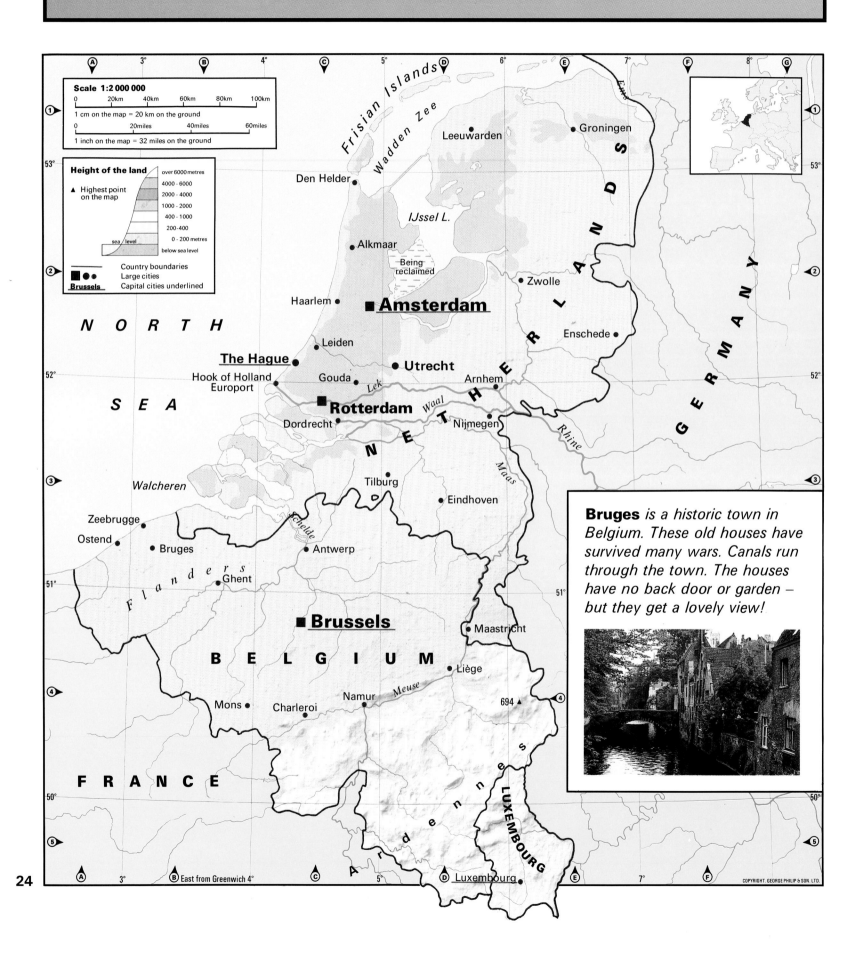

Scale 1:2 000 000

0   20km   40km   60km   80km   100km

1 cm on the map = 20 km on the ground

0   20miles   40miles   60miles

1 inch on the map = 32 miles on the ground

Height of the land

- over 6000 metres
- 4000 - 6000
- 2000 - 4000
- 1000 - 2000
- 400 - 1000
- 200-400
- 0 - 200 metres
- below sea level

▲ Highest point on the map

sea level

Country boundaries

Large cities

Brussels   Capital cities underlined

Frisian Islands

Wadden Zee

Leeuwarden   • Groningen

Den Helder

IJssel L.

• Alkmaar

Being reclaimed

• Zwolle

Haarlem •   ■**Amsterdam**

N O R T H

Enschede •

• Leiden

The Hague

• **Utrecht**

Hook of Holland   Gouda •   *Lek*   Arnhem •

Europort   ■**Rotterdam**   *Waal*

S E A

Dordrecht •   Nijmegen •

Rhine

Maas

N

Walcheren   Tilburg •

Zeebrugge •   • Eindhoven

Ostend •   • Bruges

Schelde   • Antwerp

F l a n d e r s   Ghent •

■ **Brussels**

• Maastricht

B E L G I U M

• Liège

Mons •   *Meuse*   694 ▲

Namur •

• Charleroi

F R A N C E

G E R M A N Y

N E T H E R L A N D S

A r d e n n e s

L U X E M B O U R G

• Luxembourg

Bruges *is a historic town in Belgium. These old houses have survived many wars. Canals run through the town. The houses have no back door or garden – but they get a lovely view!*

East from Greenwich

Spot the difference

What is the difference between these two coins from Belgium? And why is there a difference? (Answer on page 96.)

Europort, Rotterdam. *Rotterdam is by far the biggest port in the whole world: only a few of the docks can be seen here. Ships come from all over the world, and barges travel along the River Rhine and the canals of Europe to reach the port.*
▽

Benelux is made up from *Be*lgium, *Ne*therlands and *Lux*embourg. Fortunately, the first two letters of each name are the same in most languages, so everyone can understand the word. These three countries agreed to co-operate soon after World War 2. But they still have their own King (of Belgium), Queen (of the Netherlands) and Grand Duke (of Luxembourg).

The Benelux countries are all small and are the most crowded in mainland Europe, but there is plenty of countryside too. Most of the land is low and flat, so they are sometimes called the Low Countries. But Luxembourg and eastern Belgium have pleasant wooded hills called the Ardennes. There are lots of modern industries, but the coalfield of central Belgium is a problem area because most of the coal-mines have closed.

△
Gouda market. *See the clogs for sale among the Wellingtons and wheelbarrows! Clogs are worn by some farmers and market gardeners, but many people prefer boots for working on the marshy land.*

Are these windmills?

No, these are *not* windmills! They are really wind-*pumps*. They were used to pump water *up* from the fields into rivers and canals. The river is higher than the land! Much of the Netherlands was drained for farmland in this way. Nowadays, powerful diesel or electric pumps are used instead.

FRANCE

ATLANTIC OCEAN

UNITED KINGDOM

London

NETHERLANDS

BELGIUM

GERMANY

LUXEMBOURG

Strait of Dover

Dunkirk
Calais
Boulogne
Lille
Lens
Douai
Valenciennes

English Channel

Dieppe
Amiens
Picardy

Thionville
Metz
Lorraine
Nancy
Strasbourg

Alderney
Guernsey
Channel Islands (U.K.)
Jersey

Cherbourg
Le Havre
Rouen
Reims

Champagne

Caen

Normandy

Paris
Seine

Mulhouse
Montbéliard
Besançon

St. Malo

Chartres
Troyes

Ushant
Brest

Rennes

Brittany

Le Mans
Orléans

Dijon

Burgundy

Lorient

Angers
Tours
Loire

Bourges

SWITZERLAND

St. Nazaire
Nantes

Loire

Saône

Jura

Mt. Blanc
4807

Poitiers

Bay of Biscay

La Rochelle

Limoges

Clermont Ferrand

Lyons

Rhône

Grenoble

Angoulême

St. Étienne

Valence

ITALY

Auvergne

Massif Central

Cévennes

Rhône

Orange
Avignon

MONACO
Nice

Bordeaux
Dordogne
Garonne

Languedoc

Nîmes

Provence

Aix

Cannes

Gascony

Toulouse

Montpellier

Marseilles

Toulon

Bayonne

Carcassonne

Lourdes

Pyrenees

Perpignan

Gulf of Lions

SPAIN

ANDORRA

MEDITERRANEAN SEA

See page 32 for Corsica

Height of the land

▲ Highest point on the map

over 6000 metres	
3000 - 6000	
2000 - 3000	
1000 - 2000	
400 - 1000	
200 - 400	
sea level	0 - 200 metres
	below sea level

Country boundaries
Large cities
Paris Capital cities underlined

Scale 1:5 000 000

0   50km   100km   150km   200km   250km

1 cm on the map = 50 km on the ground

0   50miles   100miles   150miles

1 inch on the map = 80 miles on the ground

French wine

A label from a bottle of French wine. The vines are growing in long straight rows on both sides of the valley. More wine is drunk in France than in any other country.

Market at Nice. *Which vegetables can you recognize on this stall? (Answer on page 96.) Every town in France has a good market. Housewives choose fresh fruit and vegetables very carefully.*

France is a country with three coastlines: can you see which these are? It is hot in summer in the south, but it is usually cool in the mountains and in the north. France is the biggest country in Western Europe, so there are big contrasts between north and south.

The highest mountains are the Alps in the southeast and the Pyrenees in the southwest. They are popular for ski-ing in winter and for summer holidays too. More than half the country is lowland, and farming is very important. Besides fruit, vegetables and wine, France is famous for its many different cheeses.

France is changing fast. The number of people living in villages is going down, and the population of the cities is growing – partly swelled by Arabs from North Africa who have come to live in France. The biggest city is Paris, which is also the capital. Ten million people now live in the Paris region, and five big new towns have been built around Paris.

Mont Blanc. *The 'White Mountain' is the highest mountain in Western Europe. It is 4807 metres high. Even in summer (as here) it is covered in snow. Cable-cars take tourists and skiers high up the mountain.*

Made in France

These *Majorette* models are made in France. They include a Renault van, a Michelin lorry, an Air France bus and a Paris bus. The most popular French cars are:

Renault   Citroen   Peugeot

What else can you find that is made in France? In our home we have:

BIC ball-point pens
a Le Creuset frying-pan
ARCOROC glassware
ARCOPOL cups and saucers
a MOULINEX mixer
and a Philips washing machine

GERMANY AND AUSTRIA

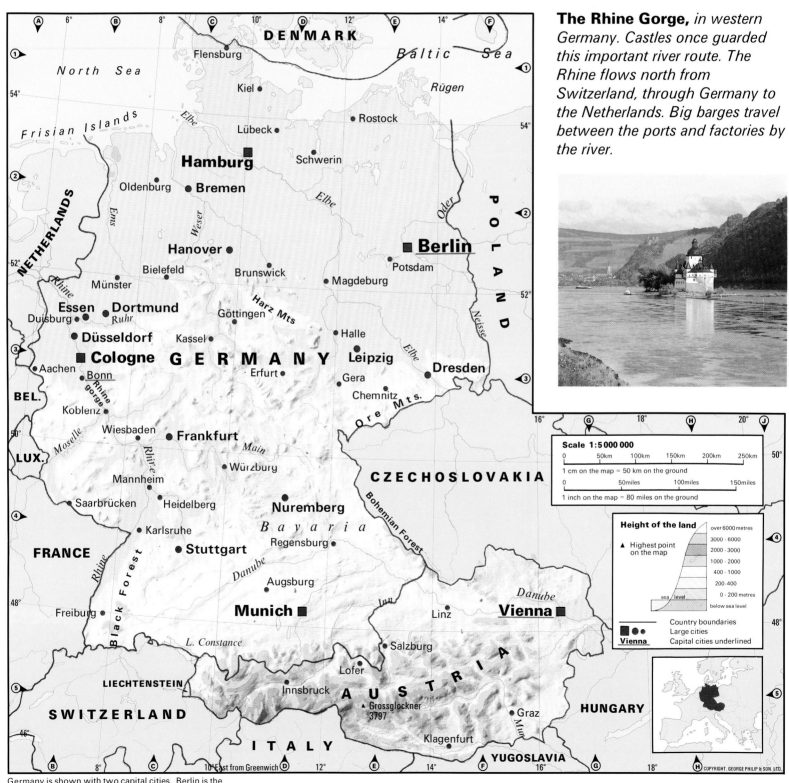

The Rhine Gorge, *in western Germany. Castles once guarded this important river route. The Rhine flows north from Switzerland, through Germany to the Netherlands. Big barges travel between the ports and factories by the river.*

DENMARK

North Sea

Baltic Sea

Flensburg

Kiel

Rügen

Lübeck • Rostock

Elbe

Hamburg

Schwerin

Frisian Islands

Oldenburg • **Bremen**

Elbe

Ems

Weser

Oder

P O L A N D

Hanover •

Bielefeld

Brunswick

Berlin

Münster

Rhine

Potsdam

NETHERLANDS

• Magdeburg

Essen Dortmund

Harz Mts

Göttingen

Neisse

Duisburg *Ruhr* •

• Halle

Düsseldorf

Kassel •

G E R M A N Y

Leipzig

Aachen •

Dresden

Cologne

Erfurt •

BEL.

Bonn

Gera •

Rhine gorge

Chemnitz •

Koblenz •

Ore Mts.

50°

Wiesbaden •

Moselle

LUX.

Frankfurt •

Main

Rhine

• Würzburg

CZECHOSLOVAKIA

Mannheim •

Saarbrücken •

Heidelberg •

Bohemian Forest

Nuremberg

FRANCE

Karlsruhe •

B a v a r i a

Regensburg •

Black Forest

Stuttgart

Danube

Rhine

Augsburg •

Freiburg •

Danube

Munich ■

Inn

Linz •

Vienna ■

LIECHTENSTEIN

L. Constance

Salzburg •

A U S T R I A

Lofer •

SWITZERLAND

Innsbruck

▲ Grossglockner
3797

• Graz

HUNGARY

Mur

Klagenfurt •

I T A L Y

YUGOSLAVIA

COPYRIGHT. GEORGE PHILIP & SON. LTD.

Scale 1:5 000 000

0   50km   100km   150km   200km   250km

1 cm on the map = 50 km on the ground

0   50miles   100miles   150miles

1 inch on the map = 80 miles on the ground

Height of the land

over 6000 metres

▲ Highest point on the map

3000 - 6000

2000 - 3000

1000 - 2000

400 - 1000

200 - 400

sea level

0 - 200 metres

below sea level

■ •• Country boundaries

Vienna Large cities

Capital cities underlined

28

Germany is shown with two capital cities. Berlin is the capital, but the seat of government is in Bonn.

Germany has more people than any other European country apart from the USSR. Most of the 80 million Germans live in towns and cities. Several million people called 'guest workers' have come from southern Europe and Turkey to work in Germany's factories. But nowadays there is unemployment in Germany, as in other European countries, and many 'guest workers' have returned home. Among the many different goods made in Germany there are excellent cars: BMW, Ford, Mercedes, Opel, Porsche, and Volkswagen.

There is also plenty of beautiful uncrowded countryside. The north is mostly lowland. Parts of the south, such as the Black Forest, are mountainous and popular for holidays.

Sausages, beer and pretzels *are popular in Germany. The beer from Munich is made from barley; the pretzels (dry biscuits) are made from wheat; the big sausages are made from pork.*

Germany was one country from 1870 to 1945. In 1990 it became one country again. From 1945 until 1990, it was divided into West Germany and East Germany, and there was a border fence between the two, with armed guards. To end World War 2 in 1945, Germany was invaded from west and east at the same time. The area occupied by the USSR forces became East Germany, with a communist government. The rest of Germany was called West Germany, even though it included southern Germany too! Now, all Germany is one country again. But its area is still smaller than it was before 1945, because all the land east of the Rivers Oder and Neisse is now in Poland.

Berlin is the capital and the biggest city of Germany. From 1945 until 1990 it was divided into two. East Berlin was the capital of East Germany, but West Berlin was still part of West Germany – even though it was surrounded by East Germany. The Berlin wall divided the city; it was knocked down in 1989.

Transport stamps

Germany has excellent railways. The stamps show two clever answers to the problems of overcrowding: a double-deck passenger train, and a monorail above the River Wupper (near the Ruhr) to save space.

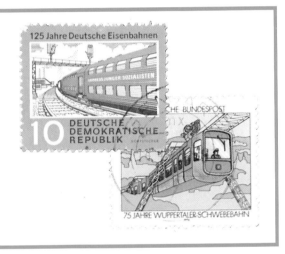

The Alps *are popular for winter sports. This guesthouse in the village of Lofer, Austria, is full of skiers in winter. Trees cover the lower slopes of the mountains: the skiers will go up to the snow-slopes above the trees.*

Austria. Until 1918, Austria and Hungary were linked, and ruled a great Empire which included much of Central Europe. But now Austria is a small, peaceful country, which is friendly with both East and West Europe.

In the west of Austria are the high Alps, and many tourists come to enjoy the beautiful scenery and winter sports. Busy motorways and electric railways cross the Austrian Alps to link Germany with Italy.

Most Austrians live in the lower eastern part of the country. The capital is Vienna. It was once near the centre of the Austrian Empire; now it is in a corner of the country.

The international clock *in Berlin, which tells the time of the whole world! It is 16.00 hours (4 pm) in Berlin: what time is it in Reykjavik (Iceland)? and in Helsinki (Finland)? And how does the clock work? (Answers on page 96.)*

SPAIN AND PORTUGAL

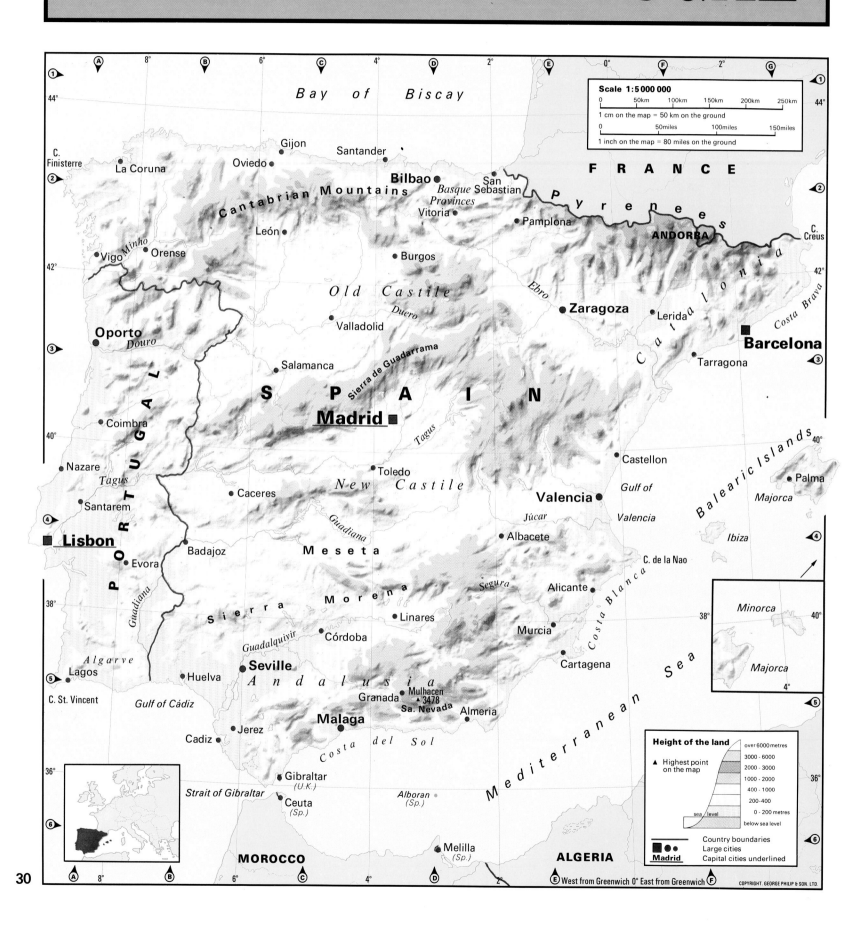

Bay of Biscay

Scale 1:5 000 000

| 0 | 50km | 100km | 150km | 200km | 250km |

1 cm on the map = 50 km on the ground

| 0 | 50miles | 100miles | 150miles |

1 inch on the map = 80 miles on the ground

C. Finisterre
La Coruna
Gijon
Santander
Oviedo
Bilbao
Basque Provinces
San Sebastian
Vitoria
Pamplona
FRANCE
Pyrenees
ANDORRA
C. Creus
León
Burgos
Cantabrian Mountains
Vigo
Minho
Orense
Old Castile
Duero
Ebro
Zaragoza
Lerida
Catalonia
Costa Brava
Oporto
Douro
Valladolid
Salamanca
Sierra de Guadarrama
SPAIN
Barcelona
Tarragona
Coimbra
PORTUGAL
Madrid
Castellon
Balearic Islands
Nazare
Tagus
New Castile
Toledo
Valencia
Gulf of Valencia
Palma
Majorca
Santarem
Caceres
Meseta
Guadiana
Júcar
Albacete
Ibiza
Lisbon
Badajoz
Evora
Guadiana
Sierra Morena
Segura
C. de la Nao
Alicante
Costa Blanca
Minorca
Algarve
Lagos
Linares
Guadalquivir
Córdoba
Murcia
Cartagena
Majorca
C. St. Vincent
Gulf of Cádiz
Huelva
Seville
Andalusia
Granada
Mulhacen
▲ 3478
Sa. Nevada
Almeria
Mediterranean Sea
Jerez
Malaga
Cadiz
Costa del Sol
Gibraltar (U.K.)
Strait of Gibraltar
Ceuta (Sp.)
Alboran (Sp.)
Melilla (Sp.)
MOROCCO
ALGERIA

Height of the land

	over 6000 metres
▲ Highest point on the map	3000 - 6000
	2000 - 3000
	1000 - 2000
	400 - 1000
	200-400
sea level	0 - 200 metres
	below sea level

Country boundaries
● ● Large cities
Madrid Capital cities underlined

30

Village in southern Spain. *The old houses crowd closely together, and roads are very narrow: wide enough for a donkey, but not for lorries. People whitewash their houses to reflect the rays of the hot sun. Olive trees grow on the hills.*

Did you know?

Gibraltar is still a British colony, but it is only 6 square kilometres in area. Spain still owns two towns in Morocco: *Ceuta* and *Melilla*. Spain wants Gibraltar – and Morocco wants Ceuta and Melilla. The arguments continue. . . .

Spain and Portugal are separated from the rest of Europe by the high Pyrenees mountains. Most people travelling by land from the north reach Spain along the Atlantic or Mediterranean coasts.

The Meseta is the high plateau of central Spain. Winters are very cold, and summers are very hot. Olives and vines are the main crops. But cars are the biggest export from Spain nowadays. Both Spain and Portugal have fine historic cities, with great churches and cathedrals – built when they were the richest countries in the world.

Spain is very popular for holidays: the Costa Brava (Rugged Coast), the Costa del Sol (Coast of the Sun), and the Balearic Islands are crowded in summer. In Portugal the Algarve coast is the most popular holiday area.

The Alhambra Palace, Granada. *This beautiful palace was built by the Moors (Arabs from North Africa). The Moors ruled southern Spain for hundreds of years, until 1492. The Arabs brought new crops and new ideas to Europe.*

Spanish coins

Spain became a monarchy again in 1975; the coin shows King Juan Carlos I.

In 1982, the World Cup was held in Spain: this special coin shows a football and the world.

Bull-ring and flats, Malaga. *The bull-ring is a big and important building in Spanish cities. High blocks of flats are typical of modern Spain. In the background is the blue Mediterranean Sea. Malaga is a large port in southern Spain.*

Sun-dried fish, Portugal. *Sardines caught in the Atlantic Ocean are dried in the strong sunshine at Nazare, Portugal. Many of the older ladies wear black clothes, even in summer.*

SWITZERLAND AND ITALY

Labels from food exported from Italy: try making a collection yourself!

Sorano, *central Italy. Long ago the hill town was a safe place to live. The houses huddled closely round the castle and the church. Nowadays, a hill town needs a zigzag road to reach it.* ▷

Italy is shaped like a boot: its toe seems to be kicking Sicily! The shape is caused by the long range of fold-mountains called the Apennines. The great Roman Empire was centred on Italy, and there are many Roman ruins. Yet Italy was only united as a country less than 150 years ago. Italy has lots of big factories. The Fiat car plant in Turin is one of the largest and most modern in the world.

△
Venice, *northeast Italy. Travel is by boat, or on foot: there are no cars, because the 'roads' are canals.*

Swiss record breakers

Switzerland holds some amazing world records.

*The *longest* road tunnel is the St Gotthard tunnel (16.32 kilometres). *The *longest* stairway is beside the Niesenbahn mountain railway, near Spiez. It has 11,674 steps! *The *steepest* railway goes up Mount Pilatus. It has a gradient of 48%.

*And Switzerland has been at peace with everyone since 1815. That's quite a record!

Switzerland also has the *oddest* car-plates: CH is from the Latin name for Switzerland:

CH

Confederatio Helvetica.

In **Switzerland** most people live in cities north of the Alps. Switzerland is one of the world's richest countries, with modern banks, offices and factories.

Rivers, dams and waterfalls in the Alps are used for making hydro-electric power: trains, factories and homes in Switzerland all run on cheap electricity. Cable-cars powered by electricity take skiers and tourists high into the beautiful mountains.

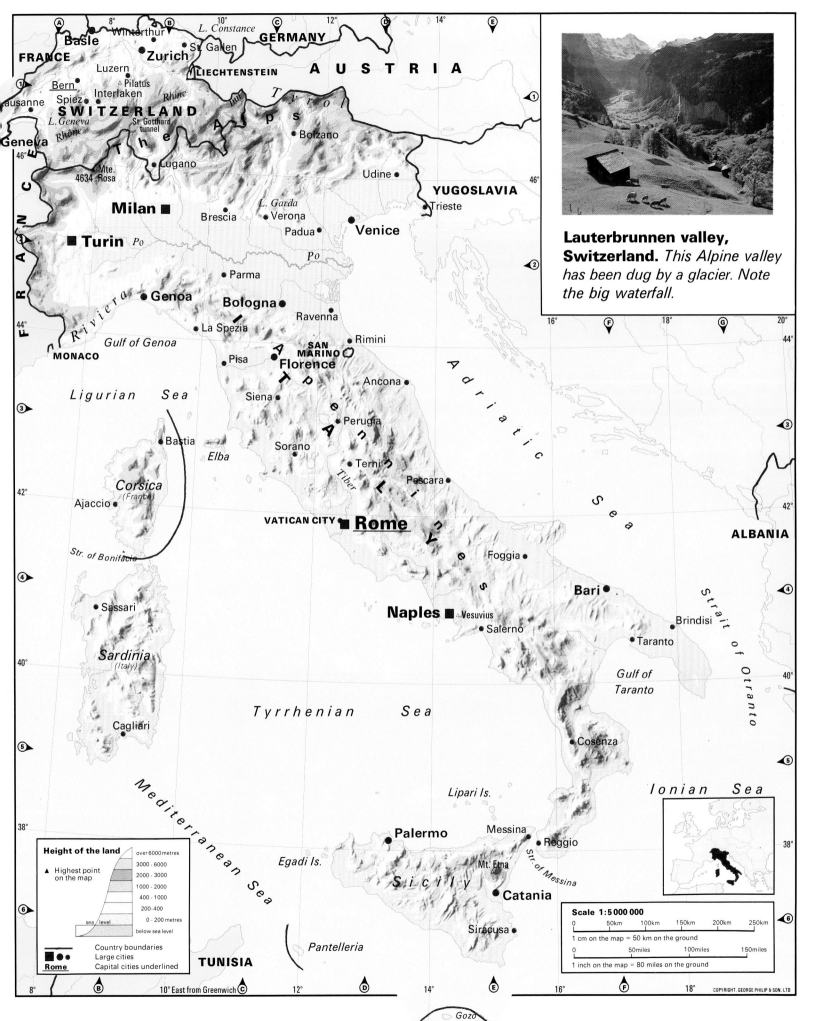

Lauterbrunnen valley, Switzerland. *This Alpine valley has been dug by a glacier. Note the big waterfall.*

A

B

Basle

FRANCE

Winterthur

8°

L. Constance

GERMANY

St Gallen

Zurich

Luzern

Pilatus

Bern

Spiez

Interlaken

Rhine

SWITZERLAND

Lausanne

L. Geneva

Rhône

Geneva

Mte.
4634 Rosa

Milan

Turin

Po

Genoa

Riviera

Gulf of Genoa

MONACO

Ligurian Sea

Bastia

Elba

Corsica
(France)

Ajaccio

Str. of Bonifacio

Sassari

Sardinia
(Italy)

Cagliari

Mediterranean Sea

LIECHTENSTEIN

AUSTRIA

Bolzano

Tyrol

The Alps

Lugano

Udine

Trieste

YUGOSLAVIA

L. Garda

Brescia

Verona

Padua

Venice

Parma

Po

Bologna

Ravenna

La Spezia

Rimini

SAN
MARINO

Pisa

Florence

Siena

Ancona

Perugia

Sorano

Terni

Tiber

Pescara

Adriatic Sea

ALBANIA

VATICAN CITY

Rome

Foggia

Bari

Brindisi

Naples

Vesuvius

Salerno

Taranto

Gulf of
Taranto

Strait of Otranto

Tyrrhenian Sea

Cosenza

Lipari Is.

Ionian Sea

Palermo

Egadi Is.

Sicily

Messina

Reggio

Mt. Etna

Str. of Messina

Catania

Siracusa

Pantelleria

TUNISIA

Height of the land

▲ Highest point on the map

over 6000 metres
3000 - 6000
2000 - 3000
1000 - 2000
400 - 1000
200 - 400
0 - 200 metres
sea level
below sea level

Country boundaries
Large cities
Capital cities underlined
Rome

Scale 1:5 000 000

0   50km   100km   150km   200km   250km

1 cm on the map = 50 km on the ground

0   50miles   100miles   150miles

1 inch on the map = 80 miles on the ground

MALTA

Gozo

Valletta

SOUTHEAST EUROPE

Most of southeast Europe is very mountainous, except near the River Danube. Farmers keep sheep and goats in the mountains and grow grain, vines and sunflowers on the lower land.

The coastlines are popular with tourists. There are many holiday resorts beside the Adriatic Sea (Yugoslavia), the Aegean Sea (Greece and Turkey) and the Black Sea (Romania and Bulgaria). All these countries are trying to develop industry, but this is still one of the poorest parts of Europe.

Albania is the least-known country in all Europe: very few people are allowed to visit it. No railways crossed the frontier of Albania until 1985.

Yugoslavia is 1 country with 2 alphabets (Latin and Cyrillic), 3 religious groups (Roman Catholic, Orthodox and Moslem), 4 languages, 6 republics and 7 neighbours (can you name them from the map?). It is the biggest country in southeast Europe.

Dubrovnik *is an old town on the coast of Yugoslavia. The walls are very big and impressive.*

Romania. *Behind the maize (sweetcorn) a huge modern factory brings jobs and money – and pollution too. The tractor and plough on the Romanian coin show that farming is still important. The Romanian language is not hard to understand. Try to read the words on the stamp.*

The Danube

The stamp shows a tourist boat at the gorge on the River Danube called the Iron Gates, on the border of Romania and Yugoslavia. The Danube flows eastwards for 1700 kilometres from West Germany to the Black Sea. It passes seven countries, and is becoming important for trade. Dams and locks now allow big ships to navigate the river.

Fishing village, Crete. *Crete is the biggest of the many islands that form part of* Greece. *The village nestles below the mountains. Some of the fishermen's cottages have become guesthouses for tourists.*

The Greek alphabet. *The Greeks developed their alphabet before the Romans, and they still use it. Some letters are the same as ours (A, B . . .), and some look the same but have a different sound (P, H . . .). The other letters are completely different. Some Greek letters appear in the Cyrillic alphabet, which is used in Bulgaria, Yugoslavia and the USSR (see page 39). The word* alphabet *is formed from the first two Greek letters:* alpha *and* beta.

A	B	Γ	Δ	E	Z	H	Θ	I	K	Λ	M	N	Ξ	O	Π	P	Σ	T	Y	Φ	X	Ψ	Ω
A	V/B	G	D	E	Z	E	TH	I	K	L	M	N	X	O	P	R	S	T	Y	F	CH	PS	O

EAST EUROPE

DENMARK

Baltic   Sea

Gdansk Bay

R.S.F.S.R.

Lithuania

● Gdansk

● Elblag

● Olsztyn

● Szczecin

● Bialystok

● Bydgoszcz

Vistula

● Torun

Bug

Warta

● Poznan

■ Warsaw

P O L A N D

● Lodz

● Radom

● Lublin

G E R M A N Y

● Wroclaw

Oder

Warta

● Kielce

● Czestochowa

S i l e s i a

● Liberec

Ohre

Vistula

● Bytom

● Gliwice

● Katowice

Labe

Prague ■

● Krakow

● Bielsko-Biala

B o h e m i a

● Ostrava

C a r p a t h i a n

Plzen ●

C Z E C H O S L O V A K I A

Olomouc ●

Telc ●

Brno ●

Morava

Tatra 2655

● Kosice

Bohemian Forest

● Bratislava

● Miskolc

A U S T R I A

Tisza

● Debrecen

● Gyor

■ Budapest

M o u n t a i n s

H U N G A R Y

Danube

L. Balaton

R O M A N I A

Y U G O S L A V I A

● Szeged

Drava

● Pecs

Tisza

Height of the land

▲ Highest point on the map

over 6000 metres
3000 - 6000
2000 - 3000
1000 - 2000
400 - 1000
200 - 400
sea level   0 - 200 metres
below sea level

Country boundaries
■ ● ● Large cities
Warsaw Capital cities underlined

Scale 1:5 000 000

0   50km   100km   150km   200km   250km

1 cm on the map = 50 km on the ground

0   50miles   100miles   150miles

1 inch on the map = 80 miles on the ground

10°   12° East from Greenwich   14°   16°   18°   20°   22°   COPYRIGHT. GEORGE PHILIP & SON. LTD.

What can you buy from Poland?

In our home, we have: shoes from Poland; chairs from Poland; books from Poland; and jam from Poland. What can *you* find from Poland?

◀ **Ploughing the fields, Poland.** *Horses are still used for ploughing fields in many parts of Poland. Look carefully . . . . How many horses are pulling the plough?*

Poland has a coastline on the Baltic Sea. There are huge shipbuilding factories at Gdansk. There are big factories in the towns in the south, too, where there is plenty of coal. Most of the country is flat farmland (see photograph).

Czechoslovakia has beautiful hills and mountains. The lower slopes are covered with pine trees. The Czechs live in the west of the country, and the Slovaks in the east. This country is the home of Skoda cars and Bata shoes.

Hungary is a small, flat country. Mostly it is farmland, but Hungary also has the biggest bus-factory in the world. Buda and Pest were twin cities, on either side of the River Danube. Now they have become Budapest, the capital city (see photograph below).

Languages. Polish, Czech and Slovak are Slavic languages. Hungarian is a totally different language; it came from central Asia. You can see some Hungarian words on the stamps and on the boat in the photograph.

The seasons in Eastern Europe:

Winter can be very cold in eastern Europe, so cross-country skiing is popular. But summers are warm and sunny. Lake Balaton is a popular holiday area in Hungary.

Budapest, Hungary: *a vintage paddle steamer on the River Danube is passing the parliament building.*

▲ **Town square in Telc, Czechoslovakia.** *The historic centres of towns are carefully preserved in Eastern Europe. Some have been totally rebuilt in the old style, after wartime bombing.*

USSR

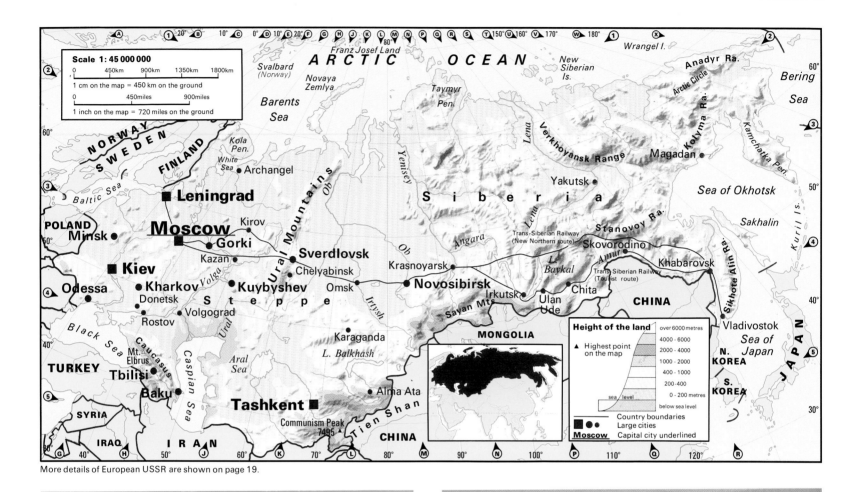

More details of European USSR are shown on page 19.

The USSR flag – the Red Flag

The hammer represents workers in industry, and the sickle represents farmworkers. The red colour represents the Communist Revolution.

USSR means
Union of
Soviet
Socialist
Republics

The USSR is by far the biggest country in the world: it is bigger than Canada and the USA together! In fact it is the biggest country in Europe *and* the biggest country in Asia as well. It is made up of 15 separate republics: the largest is Russia.

The Siberian steppes. *A lonely horse-cart travels along a track in Siberia. The steppes are* not *steps! They are part of the world's biggest plain – snow-covered in winter, and with grass or wheat in summer.*

The USSR stretches across two continents, Europe and Asia. Most people live in the European part, west of the Ural Mountains. But gradually people are moving east to new towns.

Because the USSR is so huge, there are many different climates and almost all crops can be grown. The far north is snow-covered for most of the year (see page 89). Further south is the largest forest in the world – a vast area of coniferous trees stretching from the Baltic Sea to the Sea of Okhotsk. Grassy plains, called the steppes, come south of the forest. In some parts, grain is grown on huge farms. The south is desert, hot in summer but cold in winter. With irrigation, crops like sugar-cane and cotton grow well. And in the warm hills near the Caucasus Mountains, tea is an important crop. The USSR also has huge deposits of many different minerals and can supply most of the needs of its many different factories.

The Kremlin, Moscow. *There are three former churches in the Kremlin; it now houses the government of the USSR. The golden domes can be seen far away.*

The Cyrillic alphabet

Russian is written in the Cyrillic alphabet. This is partly based on Latin letters (the same as English letters) and partly on Greek letters (see page 35).

The alphabet was invented centuries ago by St Cyril, so that the Russian church could show it was separated from both the Roman and the Greek churches. In Cyrillic, R is written P, and S is written C. So the Metro is written METPO. CCCP (on stamps and coins) is Russian for SSSR (Soyuz Sovetskikh Sotsialisticheskikh Respublik), the initials of the country in Russian.

GUM shopping centre, Moscow. *Local people go to GUM for shopping. The buildings are fine – but there are still queues and shortages in USSR shops. GUM is short for Government Department Store in Russian.*

Trans-Siberian Railway

It takes over a week to cross the USSR by train and you must change your watch seven times. Here is the distance chart and timetable (only the main stops are shown).

Distance in km	Town	Time (at Moscow)	Day
0	Moscow	14.30	1
957	Kirov	06.16	2
1818	Sverdlovsk	19.40	2
2716	Omsk	09.48	3
3343	Novosibirsk	19.55	3
4104	Krasnoyarsk	08.49	4
5184	Irkutsk	04.45	5
5647	Ulan Ude	13.07	5
6204	Chita	23.17	5
7313	Skovorodino	22.27	6
8531	Khabarovsk	22.35	7
9297	Vladivostok	13.15*	8

*This is 20.05 local time at Vladivostok.

Don't forget to allow another 8 days if you want to come back!

А	Б	В	Г	Д	Е	Ё	Ж	З	И	Й	К	Л	М	Н	О	П	Р	С	Т	У	Ф	Х	Ц	Ч	Ш	Щ	Ъ	Э	Ю	Я
A	B	V	G	D	E	YO	ZH	Z	I	Y	K	L	M	N	O	P	R	S	T	U	F	KH	TS	CH	SH	SHCH	—	E	YU	YA

ASIA

Asia is the world's biggest continent, stretching from the cold Arctic Ocean in the north, to the warm Indian Ocean in the tropical south. Mainland Asia nearly reaches the Equator in Malaysia. Several Asian islands are *on* the Equator: Sumatra, Borneo and Sulawesi. In the west, Asia reaches Europe and the Mediterranean Sea, and in the east Asia reaches the Pacific Ocean, and gets close to Australia. In the centre are the high, empty plateaus of Tibet and Mongolia.

◁ **Himalayan Mountains, Nepal,** *photographed by the famous mountaineer Chris Bonington. The world's ten highest mountains are all in the Himalayas. Glaciers have carved the deep valleys.*

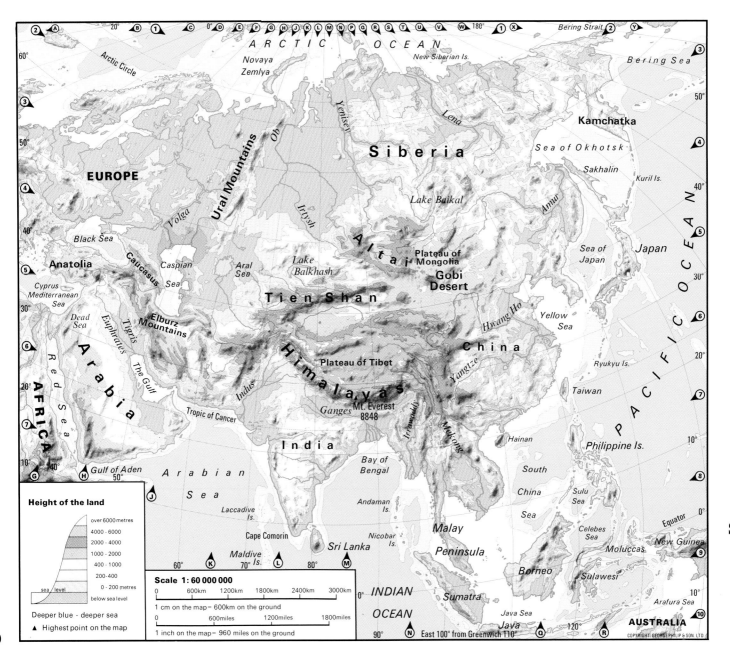

Height of the land

- over 6000 metres
- 4000 - 6000
- 2000 - 4000
- 1000 - 2000
- 400 - 1000
- 200 - 400
- 0 - 200 metres
- sea level
- below sea level

Deeper blue - deeper sea

▲ Highest point on the map

Scale 1 : 60 000 000

| 0 | 600km | 1200km | 1800km | 2400km | 3000km |

1 cm on the map = 600km on the ground

| 0 | 600miles | 1200miles | 1800miles |

1 inch on the map = 960 miles on the ground

East 100° from Greenwich

Money in Asian

Afghanistan
Bangladesh
Bhutan
Burma
Cambodia
China
Cyprus
Indonesia
Iran
Israel
Japan
Korea, N
and S
Laos
Lebanon
Syria
Macao
Maldives
Mongolia
Oman
Philippines
Qatar
Saudi Arabia
Sri Lanka
Thailand
Turkey
UAE
Vietnam

COPYRIGHT GEORGE PHILIP & SON LTD

Fact box: Asia

Area 44,387,000 square kilometres (including Asiatic USSR)
Highest point Mount Everest* (Nepal/China), 8848 metres
Lowest point Shores of Dead Sea* (Israel/Jordan), 400 metres below sea-level
Longest river Yenisey (USSR), 5540 kilometres; Yangtze (China), 5530 kilometres
Biggest country USSR* 22,402,200 square kilometres
Smallest country The Maldives, 298 square kilometres
*A *world record* as well as an Asian record

Buddhist shrine. *Religion is very important to most people in Asia. This Buddhist shrine is like many found in Nepal. It has been decorated with prayer flags and painted eyes.* ▷

Two countries cover over half of Asia: the USSR and China. India looks quite small – yet it is over ten times as big as Italy or the UK! But some of Asia's important countries are very small indeed, for example Lebanon and Israel in southwest Asia (Middle East); Singapore and Brunei in southeast Asia (Far East).

Over half the world's population lives in Asia. The coastal areas of south and east Asia are the most crowded parts. Seven of the 'top ten' most populated countries in the world are in Asia: China, India, USSR, Indonesia, Japan, Bangladesh and Pakistan.

some countries

Afghani
Taka
Ngultrum
Kyat
Riel
Yuan
Pound
Rupiah
Rial
Shekel
Yen

Won
Kip

Pound
Pataca
Rufiyaa
Tugrik
Omani
Peso
Riyal
Rial
Rupee
Baht
Lira
Dirham
Dong

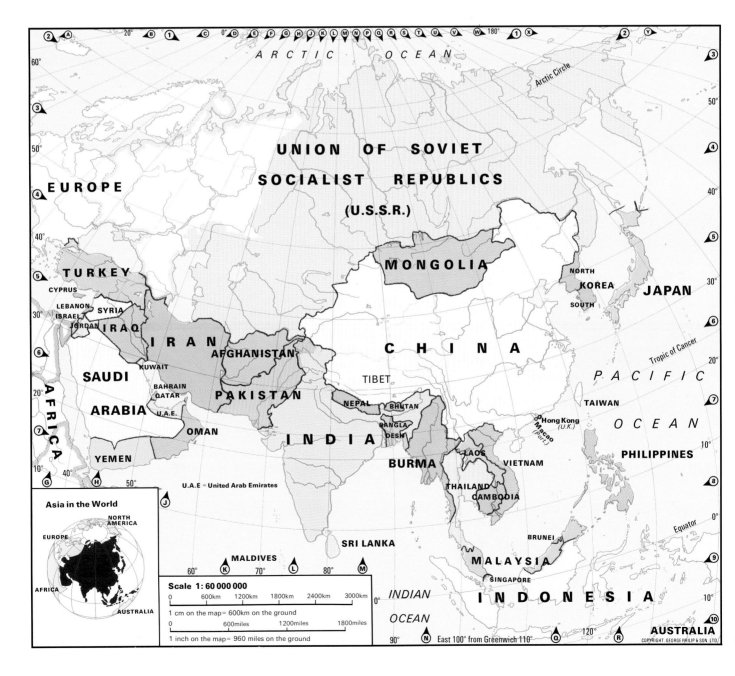

Asia in the World

Scale 1: 60 000 000

1 cm on the map = 600km on the ground
1 inch on the map = 960 miles on the ground

U.A.E = United Arab Emirates

East 100° from Greenwich

COPYRIGHT GEORGE PHILIP & SON, LTD.

MIDDLE EAST

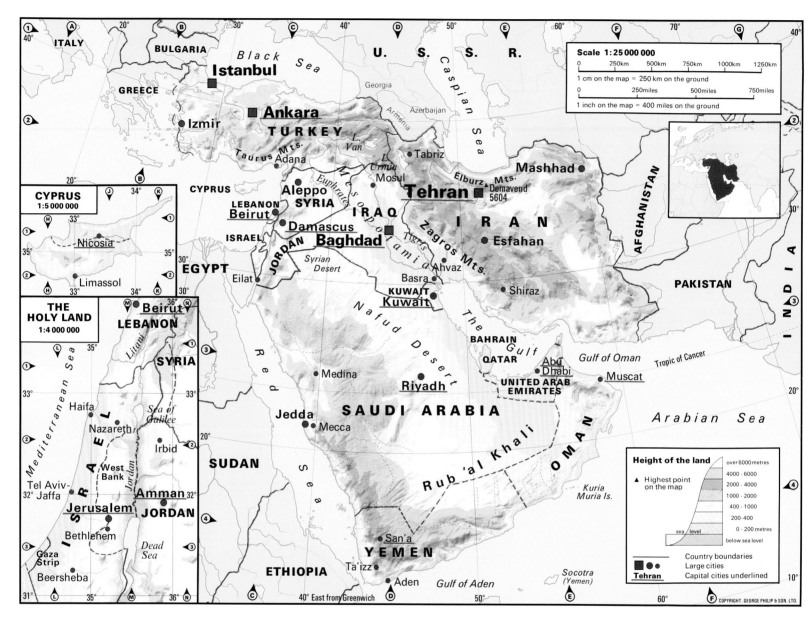

Scale 1:25 000 000

1 cm on the map = 250 km on the ground

1 inch on the map = 400 miles on the ground

CYPRUS
1:5 000 000

Nicosia

Limassol

THE HOLY LAND
1:4 000 000

Height of the land
- over 6000 metres
- 4000 - 6000
- 2000 - 4000
- 1000 - 2000
- 400 - 1000
- 200 - 400
- 0 - 200 metres
- below sea level

▲ Highest point on the map

— Country boundaries
■ ● ● Large cities
Tehran Capital cities underlined

◁ **Holy cities of the Middle East.**
In Jerusalem (*left*), Jews worship at the Wailing Wall, all that remains of the Jewish temple. *Jerusalem* is a holy city for people of three religions: Judaism, Christianity and Islam. People of all three religions live here and pilgrims and tourists visit the city.

Mecca (*right*) is the holiest city of ▷ Islam: it is where the prophet Mohammed was born. Moslems come from many countries to worship here.

Lands of the books

Three great religions started in the Middle East: Judaism, Christianity and Islam.

The Jewish scriptures are written in Hebrew. This is the world's oldest written language still in use today and reads from right to left across the page.

The Christian Bible consists of the Jewish scriptures (the Old Testament), plus the New Testament, which was originally written in Greek.

The Koran is the holy book of Islam. It is written in Arabic, which is also read from right to left.

The Jewish scriptures are written in Hebrew. ▽

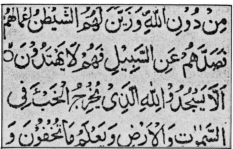

The Koran is written in Arabic. ▽

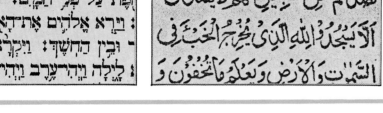

The 'Middle East' is another name for 'southwest Asia'. It is the part of Asia which is closest to Europe and Africa. In fact, Turkey is partly in Europe. Of all the countries on this map, Turkey has the most people.

Most of the Middle East is semi-desert or desert. Yet many great civilizations have existed here, such as the Assyrian, the Babylonian and the Persian. Their monuments are found in the fertile valleys of the largest rivers, the Tigris and the Euphrates.

Scarce water is used to irrigate crops in some places. In others, herds of sheep and goats are kept. Dates from Iraq come from desert oases; oranges come from irrigated land in Israel.

△

Oil in the Middle East. *The photograph above, taken in Iran, shows camels in the desert . . . a view that has not changed for centuries. But the flares and smoke in the distance are a clue to the biggest change in the Middle East: oil. Oil is pumped out from deep underground, and piped to ports for export to many countries in Europe, Asia and Africa. It is used for diesel, petroleum, paraffin and chemicals.*

△

Progress in Qatar. *The big bulldozer was imported from England, to help build the new road. In the background you can see new skyscrapers and a big crane. Oil has made some countries in the Middle East very rich, especially those near The Gulf, like Saudi Arabia, Kuwait and Qatar.*

◁ **Winnowing wheat in Turkey.** *The gentle evening breeze separates the grain from the chaff: the heavier grain falls down, while the lighter chaff blows away. Winnowing is hard work! It has been done by hand for thousands of years: the old methods are still commonly used in many parts of the Middle East.*

43

SOUTH ASIA

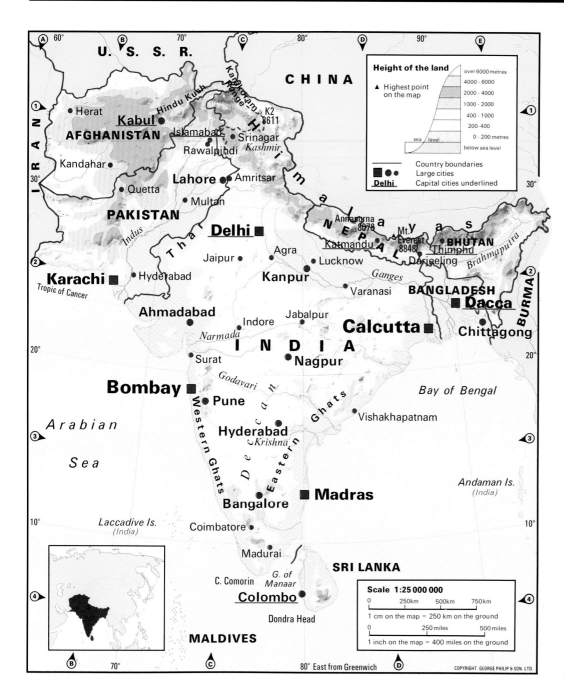

The world's highest mountains appear on this map, including Mount Everest. The Himalayas form a great mountain chain which joins on to other high mountain areas, such as the Hindu Kush.

Afghanistan is a rugged and mountainous country. Five other countries share the peninsula which stretches southwards from the Himalayas. **Bhutan** and **Nepal** are small mountain kingdoms.

Bangladesh is quite different: it is mostly flat, low-lying land where the great rivers Ganges and Brahmaputra reach the sea. In the west, **Pakistan** is a desert country, but the River Indus is used to irrigate crops.

India is the largest country. It stretches 3300 kilometres from Kashmir to Cape Comorin. Until 1947, Pakistan and Bangladesh were part of the Indian Empire, ruled by Britain.

Sri Lanka is an island country off the south coast of India. Further south, in the Indian Ocean, a chain of islands makes up the country called **The Maldives.**

More than 1000 million people live in south Asia. The deserts and mountains do not have many people, but the river valleys, plains and plateaus are crowded.

Sri Lanka *means Resplendent Isle. This country used to be called Ceylon.*

CEYLON TEA

Tea is an important crop in the hills where there is plenty of rain. Women pick the young leaves from the bushes (right)*, then they are dried and crushed and packed into tea-chests. Ceylon tea* (left) *is one of Sri Lanka's most important exports. Where does the tea you drink come from?*

△
Planting rice, Bangladesh. *These men are planting out rice seedlings in the wet soil. Sometimes monsoon floods can wash away the seedlings.*

Rice is an important food crop in south Asia. It grows best where the land is flat, and where the weather is hot and wet. The seeds are planted in a 'nursery' bed just before the monsoon rains are due (see below). When the fields are flooded, the seedlings are planted in the mud. In a good year, rice grows in the wet fields and is ready for harvesting after four or five months. If the monsoon fails and there is a drought, the seedlings will shrivel up. If the rice crop fails, many people go hungry. In areas where irrigation is available, the farmer can control the water supply and may be able to grow two rice crops a year.

Religion is very important in the lives of people in south Asia. Hinduism is the oldest religion, and most people in India and Nepal are Hindus. Buddhism began in India, but only Sri Lanka and Bhutan are mainly Buddhist today. Afghanistan, Pakistan and Bangladesh are Islamic countries. Many Sikhs live in northern India; there are also Christian groups in all these countries.

India's flag *shows that people of different religions are united in one country. The orange stripe is for Hindus; the green for Moslems; and the white for peace, with the wheel of Ashoka for Buddhists.*

Wool for carpets. *This lady in northern India is winding wool which will be used to make carpets. She sits in the courtyard of her house, where the ploughs and pots and pans are also kept.*
▽

The monsoon

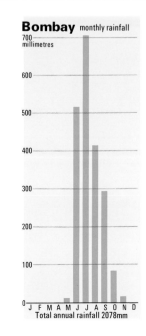

Bombay monthly rainfall

Most rain falls in one season, called the monsoon. In Bombay the monsoon begins in June (*left*) and the rain pours down for a few weeks (*right*). There are heavy showers in August and September, and then hardly any more rain until next June. From October to March the weather is cool and dry, then it gets hotter and hotter until the monsoon rains begin.

Northeast India and Bangladesh have even more rain than Bombay. But large areas of northwest India are desert.

SOUTHEAST ASIA

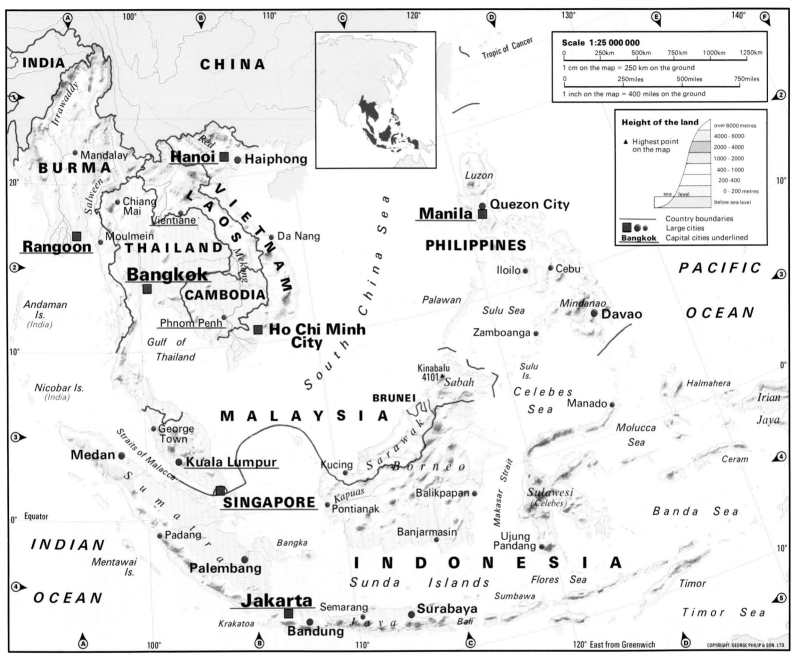

INDIA

CHINA

Tropic of Cancer

Scale 1:25 000 000

| 0 | 250km | 500km | 750km | 1000km | 1250km |

1 cm on the map = 250 km on the ground

| 0 | 250miles | 500miles | 750miles |

1 inch on the map = 400 miles on the ground

Height of the land

	over 6000 metres
▲ Highest point on the map	4000 - 6000
	2000 - 4000
	1000 - 2000
	400 - 1000
	200-400
sea level	0 - 200 metres
	below sea level

Country boundaries
Large cities
Bangkok Capital cities underlined

Irrawaddy

Mandalay

BURMA

20°

Red

Hanoi ● Haiphong

Luzon

Salween

Chiang Mai

LAOS

VIETNAM

Vientiane

Da Nang

Manila ● **Quezon City**

Rangoon

THAILAND

Mekong

PHILIPPINES

South China Sea

2°

Moulmein

Iloilo ● ● Cebu

PACIFIC

Bangkok

CAMBODIA

Andaman Is. (India)

Phnom Penh

Palawan

Sulu Sea

Mindanao ● **Davao**

OCEAN

Ho Chi Minh City

Zamboanga ●

Gulf of Thailand

10°

Nicobar Is. (India)

Kinabalu 4101▲ *Sabah*

Sulu Is.

Celebes Sea

Halmahera

BRUNEI

Manado ●

Irian Jaya

3°

M A L A Y S I A

Sarawak

Molucca Sea

Ceram

● George Town

Straits of Malacca

Medan ●

Kuala Lumpur

Kucing

Borneo

Makasar Strait

Sulawesi (Celebes)

Banda Sea

Sumatra

SINGAPORE

Kapuas

● Pontianak

Balikpapan ●

0° Equator

● Padang

Banjarmasin ●

Ujung Pandang ●

Mentawai Is.

Bangka

I N D O N E S I A

INDIAN

Palembang

Flores Sea

Timor

4°

OCEAN

Sunda Islands

Sumbawa

Timor Sea

Jakarta Semarang

● **Surabaya**

Krakatoa

Java

Bali

Bandung

120° East from Greenwich

COPYRIGHT. GEORGE PHILIP & SON. LTD.

Stamps from Southeast Asia.
Singapore *has four main religions:*

Christian   Buddhist   Islamic   Hindu
church   temple   mosque   temple

Laos. *Elephants carry huge logs from the jungle. Laos was once called Lanxang – 'land of a million elephants'.*

Vietnam. *Children learn to draw their country. North and South Vietnam were united in 1976 after many years of fighting.*

46

The Equator crosses Southeast Asia, so it is always hot. Heavy tropical rainstorms are common, too.

The mainland and most of the islands are very mountainous. The mountains are covered with thick tropical forest (look at the stamp of Laos). These areas are very difficult to reach and have few people. The large rivers are important routes inland. Their valleys and deltas are very crowded indeed.

Indonesia is the biggest country. It used to be the Dutch East Indies.

The Philippines is another large group of islands, south of China. They were Spanish until 1898.

Malaysia includes part of the mainland and most of northern Borneo.

Singapore is an island at the tip of mainland Malaysia, but a separate country. Both countries were once British and Singapore still belongs to the Commonwealth.

Burma was part of the Indian Empire. It became independent in 1948.

Vietnam, Laos and **Cambodia** were once called French Indo-China. The full name of Laos is written in French on the stamp.

Thailand has always been independent, and has a king. It used to be called Siam.

Floating market in Thailand.
Farmers bring their fruit and vegetables to Bangkok market by boat. On some boats there are fish which are cooked on the boat and sold for lunch.

Harvesting rice. *Rice grows on terraces cut into the mountainside in Bali. Each terrace is sown and harvested by hand. Bali is a small island east of Java. Some people claim that it is the most beautiful island of Indonesia, and all the world!*

A Thai schoolbook. *This page from a children's book about Thailand shows a man harvesting pineapples. Can you see how he waters the fields from the river?*

Fact box: Indonesia
Did you know that Indonesia: has the **fifth largest population** in the world (see page 9); is the **world's greatest archipelago** – a group of 13,000 islands, which stretches for 5600 kilometres; has **more active volcanoes** than any other country (77); suffered the **world's biggest recorded bang** – when the island of Krakatoa blew up in a volcanic eruption in 1883.

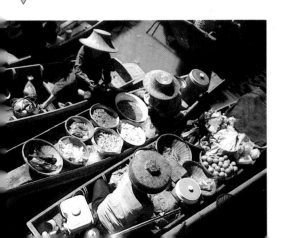

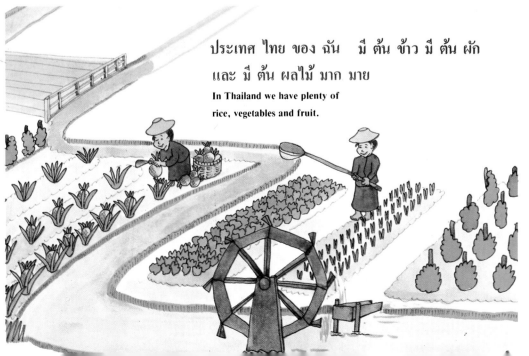

ประเทศ ไทย ของ ฉัน มี ต้น ข้าว มี ต้น ผัก
และ มี ต้น ผลไม้ มาก มาย
In Thailand we have plenty of rice, vegetables and fruit.

47

CHINA
AND NEIGHBOURS

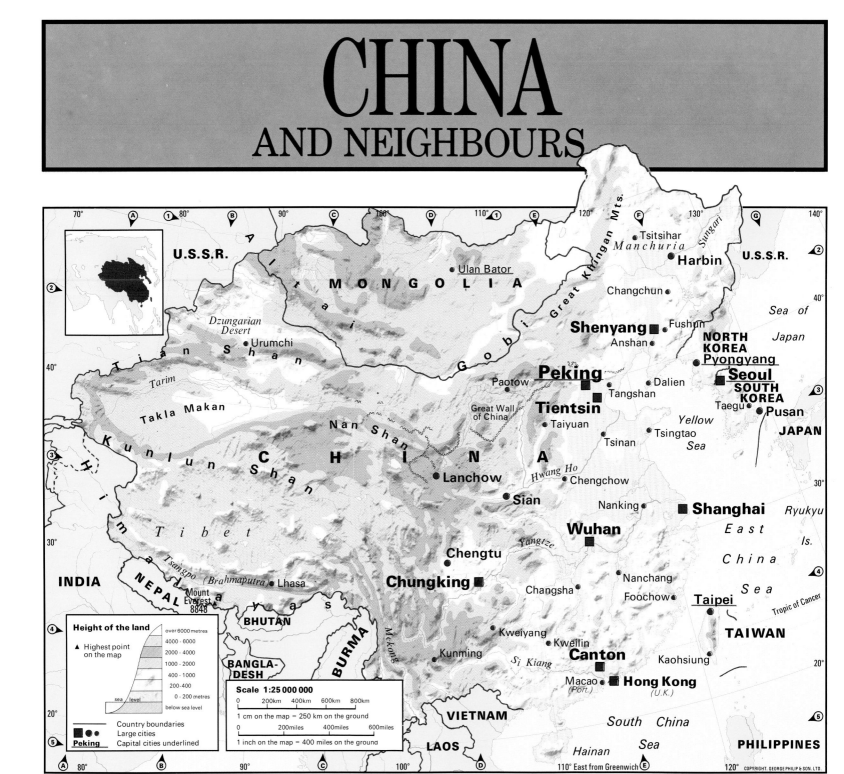

China's amazing mountains. *Both the stamp and the photograph show the amazing shapes of the limestone mountains in southern China. The mountains that look 'unreal' in Chinese paintings really are real! It is almost impossible to travel through this area except by boat. The heavy rain has slowly dissolved the limestone to make these picturesque mountains. They are now one of China's main tourist attractions. The river is the Kwei which flows through Kweilin, an old city dating back to the sixth century.*

China has over a billion people (1,000,000,000) — more than any other country in the world. The map shows that there are many high mountains in China, such as the huge plateau of Tibet and the rugged mountains of the southwest where the Giant Pandas live. Not many people live in these mountains, nor in the deserts of the north, near Mongolia. So the lower land of eastern China is *very* crowded indeed. Rice grows well south of the River Yangtze. North of the Yangtze, where the winters are colder, wheat and maize are important food crops, but it is hard to grow enough.

Building a reservoir. *Everybody, male and female, pulls a heavy cart of rocks to make a new dam across a river. The dam will provide water for power and for irrigation — and it will control flooding too. China has made great progress with projects like this, which use lots of people and few machines. Long ago the Great Wall of China was built in this way to keep out China's enemies.*

China's neighbours

Mongolia is a huge desert country, three times bigger than Spain. It is the world's emptiest country: there are fewer than 3 million people.

North Korea is a communist country. It separated from South Korea in the Korean War in 1953.

South Korea has over 43 million people – more than Canada and Australia put together!

Taiwan is an island country which used to be called Formosa, or nationalist China. It is not communist and is not part of the rest of China.

Hong Kong will be a British colony until 1997, when the land will be handed back to China. Big new skyscrapers stand on the hills to fit 6 million people into a crowded island. The hydrofoil is going to **Macao**, a nearby Portuguese colony.

Traffic in Tientsin. *Rush hour in Chinese cities is not the same as in New York or London: there are hardly any cars. People travel on foot, or by bicycle or bus. Tientsin is a big port in northern China and is one of the largest cities in the country.*

Fact box

* One person out of every five people in the world is Chinese.

* This century's worst earthquake happened in Tangshan in 1976. This is in the crowded part of China, so many people were killed.

* The Chinese invented an earthquake detector 1800 years ago. They also invented the compass, paper and printing.

* The place furthest from the open sea is in China: the Dzungarian Desert, 2400 kilometres from the sea. A man from Norwich in England who cycled there said it is 'hot and horrible'!

* The highest plateau in the world is Tibet. Its average height is nearly 5000 metres above sea-level – as high as Mont Blanc (see page 27)! Lhasa, Tibet, has the world's highest airport, at 4363 metres. The runway is extra long as there is so little air pressure to help aircraft take off.

* The Chinese language has many dialects: the commonest is Mandarin. Each sound has four tones; words are written using thousands of different characters. Chinese used to be written from top to bottom of the page; now it is written from left to right.

JAPAN

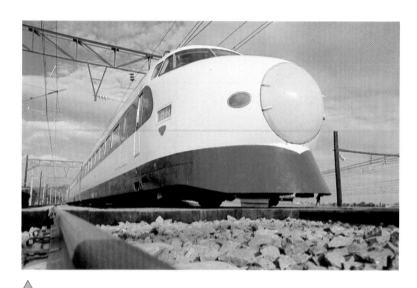

Bullet train. *Japan's 'bullet trains' go like a bullet from a gun! The trains run on new tracks with no sharp curves to slow them down. They provide a superb service except when there is an earthquake warning. When that happens, the trains have to go more slowly, to be safe.*

Japan is quite a small country: it is smaller than France or Spain. Canada is twenty-seven times as big as Japan! But Japan has a big population – about 124,000,000. This is over twice as many people as France, and five times as many as Canada.

People talk of the 'Japanese miracle'. This small country is mostly mountains, has very few mines and hardly any oil, yet it has become the world's biggest producer of televisions, radios, music centres, cameras, trucks, ships and many other things. Japanese cars and computers are admired throughout the world. There are booming cities in the south of Japan, with highly skilled, hard-working people. But most of Japan is still peaceful and beautiful.

In the south rice is the main food crop. Some of the hillsides look like giant steps, because they are terraced to make flat fields for growing rice.

Mount Fuji in winter. *Fujiyama (Mount Fuji) is Japan's most famous mountain. It is an old volcano, 3776 metres high. In winter, the upper slopes are snow-covered. The 'bullet trains' pass Mount Fuji on their high-speed journey from Tokyo to Nagoya and Osaka.*

Huge baskets for live fish. *Fish are caught and then stored in these huge baskets. The Japanese eat more fish than people in any other country, but sadly the seas near Japan have been polluted by industry. Big Japanese trawlers now fish thousands of kilometres away from home.*

Many mountains are volcanoes. There are 54 active volcanoes, and over 100 others (see below). The northernmost island, Hokkaido, is much less crowded. It has very cold winters, and even the summers are too cold for growing rice.

Horyu Temple, at Nara

The beautiful temple on the right is called a pagoda. Japanese pagodas are carefully preserved. Their unusual shape originally came partly from Indian temples and partly from Chinese temples. This is one of many Japanese stamps on the theme of national treasures. You could collect them.

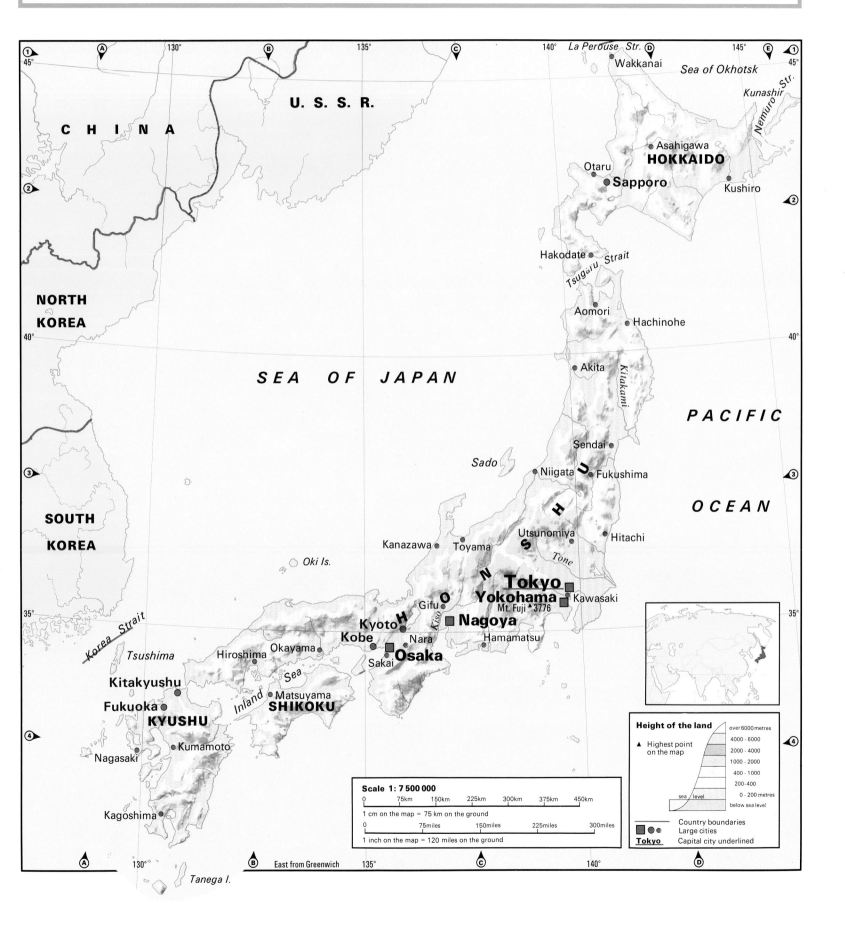

La Perouse Str.

Wakkanai

Sea of Okhotsk

Kunashir Str.

U. S. S. R.

C H I N A

Nemuro Str.

Asahigawa

HOKKAIDO

Otaru

Sapporo

Kushiro

NORTH KOREA

Hakodate
Tsugaru Strait

Aomori
Hachinohe

40°

Akita

Kitakami

S E A   O F   J A P A N

Sado

Sendai

Niigata
Fukushima

PACIFIC

SOUTH KOREA

O C E A N

Kanazawa
Toyama

Utsunomiya
Hitachi

Oki Is.

Tone

Tokyo
Yokohama
Kawasaki

Kyoto
Gifu

Mt. Fuji ▲ 3776

Korea Strait

Kobe
Nara
Nagoya

Tsushima

Okayama
Sakai
Osaka
Hamamatsu

Hiroshima

Inland Sea

Matsuyama

SHIKOKU

Kitakyushu

Fukuoka

KYUSHU

Kumamoto

Nagasaki

Kagoshima

Scale 1: 7 500 000

| 0 | 75km | 150km | 225km | 300km | 375km | 450km |

1 cm on the map = 75 km on the ground

| 0 | 75miles | 150miles | 225miles | 300miles |

1 inch on the map = 120 miles on the ground

Height of the land

▲ Highest point on the map

over 6000 metres
4000 - 6000
2000 - 4000
1000 - 2000
400 - 1000
200 - 400
0 - 200 metres
below sea level

sea level

Country boundaries
Large cities
Capital city underlined

Tokyo

East from Greenwich

Tanega I.

130°   135°   140°   145°

45°   40°   35°

AFRICA

◁ **Children in Ghana.** *Everywhere in Africa, there are lots of children. The fathers of these children are fishermen: in the background you can see big dug-out canoes. The canoes are made from the huge trees of the rain-forest, and can cope with big waves in the Gulf of Guinea. These children get plenty of fish to eat, but in some parts of Africa hunger is a major problem.*

Most of the countries of Africa have quite small populations – except for Nigeria and Egypt. But everywhere the population is growing fast. It is difficult to provide enough schools and clinics for all the children and there are not enough good jobs. So African countries are trying hard to improve fishing, mining, and industry.

Fact box: Africa

Area 30,319,000 square kilometres

Highest point Mount Kilimanjaro (Tanzania), 5895 metres

Lowest point Shores of Lake Assal (Djibouti), 155 metres below sea-level

Longest river Nile, 6670 kilometres (also a *world* record)

Largest lake Lake Victoria (East Africa), 69,484 square kilometres

Biggest country Sudan, 2,505,813 square kilometres

Smallest country *Mainland:* Gambia, 11,295 square kilometres; *islands:* Seychelles, 308 square kilometres (see p. 9)

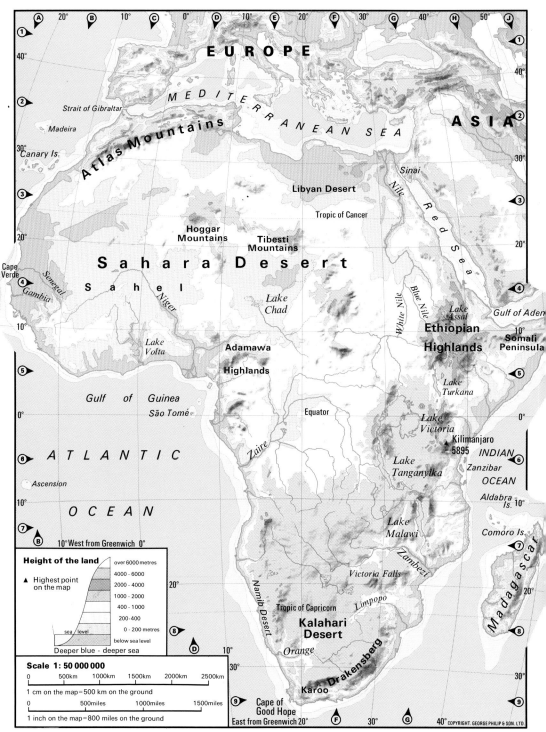

◀ **The pyramids of Egypt.** *The pyramids are tombs which were built by slaves over 4000 years ago. They are still the biggest buildings in the whole of Africa. They are near the River Nile, in the Sahara desert.*

These camels are for the tourists that visit the pyramids.

Imagine travelling southwards across Africa, along the 20°E line of longitude. You start in Libya. Your first 1000 kilometres will be across the great Sahara desert (where you *must* travel in winter) – sand, rock and the high rugged Tibesti Mountains. Then you reach thorn bushes, in the semi-desert Sahel area of Chad.

By 15°N you are into savanna – very long grass and scattered trees. You cross the country known as CAR for short. The land becomes greener and at about 5°N you reach the equatorial rain-forest . . . a real jungle! You are now in Zaïre.

Then the same story happens in reverse – savanna in Angola; then semi-desert (the Kalahari and the Karoo). Finally you reach the mountains and coast of South Africa – a journey of nearly 8000 kilometres.

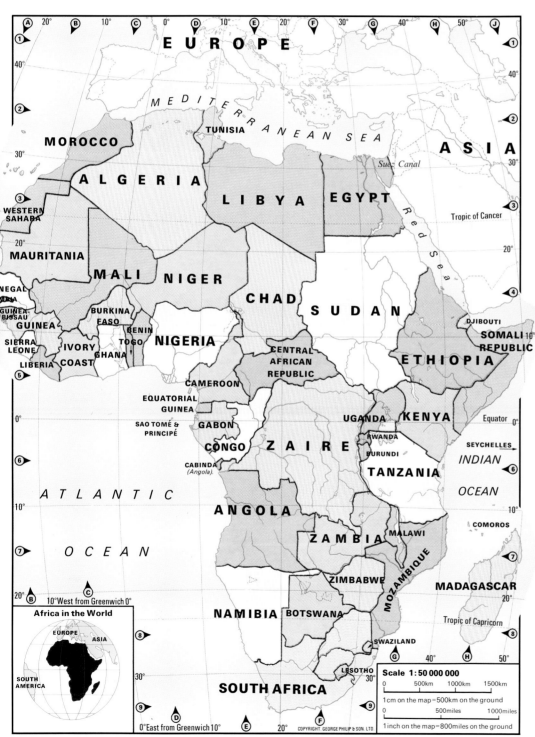

Where do the country names come from?

Ghana, Benin, Mali
Names of great empires in West Africa a long time ago

Gambia, Niger, Nigeria
From big rivers in these countries

Chad From Lake Chad

Namibia From the *Namib* desert

Tanzania From *Tan*ganyika (the mainland) and the island of *Zan*zibar

Sierra Leone 'Lion Mountain' in Portuguese (named by explorers)

Ivory Coast Ivory, from the tusks of elephants, used to be traded along this coast

NORTH AFRICA

Most of North Africa is desert – but not all. The coastlines and mountains of northwest Africa get winter rain: good crops are grown, and the area is popular all year with tourists from Europe. These countries are Islamic. **Morocco** has the oldest university in the world: the Islamic University in Fez.

Oil has made **Libya** rich. The other countries still have much poverty. The Sahel states, at the southern edge of the Sahara, are among the poorest countries in the world. They had severe famines in the 1970s and 1980s.

Egypt has the biggest population of any North African country. Its capital, Cairo, is one of the biggest cities in the world. The River Nile brings water to the valley and delta. The land is carefully farmed (with irrigation) and crowded with people; the rest of Egypt is almost empty. The map shows that part of the desert is *below* sea-level.

The lack of rain has helped to preserve many of the marvellous monuments, palaces and tombs built by the ancient Egyptians. The pyramids at Giza, near Cairo, are 4500 years old (see page 53). They are the only one of the Seven Wonders of the ancient world still surviving.

◁ **Oasis, Algeria.** *The water allows date-palms to grow well. But in the background, great sand-dunes loom on the skyline: if they advance, they may cover the oasis one day. In the foreground there is rock desert – that is more common than sand desert.*

Huge sand-dunes, Libya. *Land-Rover tracks can be seen in the foreground. But no vehicles can cross the huge, steep sand-dunes in the background. The Land-Rover has stopped in front of the dunes. Only about a tenth of the Sahara desert is made up of sand-dunes. Other parts are gravel desert, rock desert, salt desert, dried-up lakes, and desert mountains.*
▽

△
Camels at market, Tunisia. *Camels are ideal for deserts: they can survive for a long time without water, by relying on the fat in their humps. They can carry heavy loads, and can walk well on soft sand. But nowadays, lorries are taking over from camels for long-distance travel.*

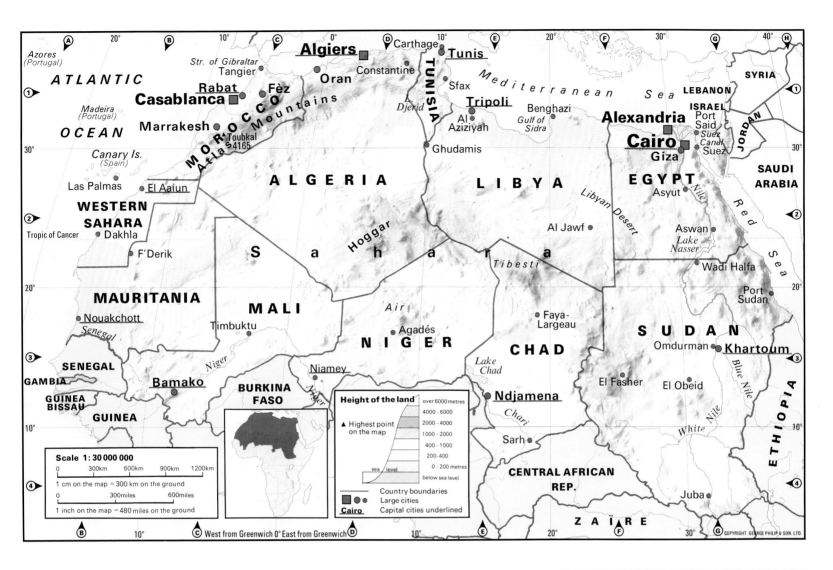

Height of the land

	over 6000 metres
	4000 - 6000
▲ Highest point on the map	2000 - 4000
	1000 - 2000
	400 - 1000
	200-400
	0 - 200 metres
sea / level	below sea level

Country boundaries
■ ● ● Large cities
<u>Cairo</u> Capital cities underlined

Scale 1 : 30 000 000

0 300km 600km 900km 1200km
1 cm on the map = 300 km on the ground
0 300miles 600miles
1 inch on the map = 480 miles on the ground

West from Greenwich 0° East from Greenwich

COPYRIGHT. GEORGE PHILIP & SON. LTD.

Puzzle picture

This is a satellite photograph of part of the Sahara desert in southern Libya. Who has drawn these circles in the desert, and why? How have they become green? Why are some circles more green than others?

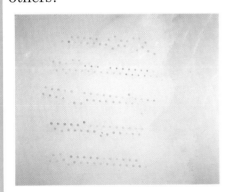

Have a guess – then turn to page 96.

The Suez Canal. *This container ship is travelling through the desert of Egypt! The Suez Canal was dug in 1859–69 by Arabs, organized by a Frenchman, Ferdinand de Lesseps. Before the canal was dug, the route from Europe to India and the Far East was round the whole of Africa.*

For almost a century, the canal was a very important route; but now aeroplanes have taken over almost all the passenger traffic, and many oil-tankers are much too big to go through it. Today it is mostly used for freight travelling from Asia to Europe.

▽

Saharan records

The Sahara is the **biggest desert** in the world. It is over 8 million square kilometres in size. From west to east it is over 5000 kilometres; from north to south it extends about 2000 kilometres and it is still growing.

The **hottest shade temperature** ever recorded, 58°C, was in Al Aziziyah, Libya, in 1922.

The **sunniest** place in the world, over 4300 hours of sunshine per year, is in the eastern Sahara.

The **highest sand-dunes** in the world, 430 metres high, are in east central Algeria.

The **longest river** in the world is the River Nile, 6670 kilometres. (How strange that a desert should have the world's longest river!)

WEST AFRICA

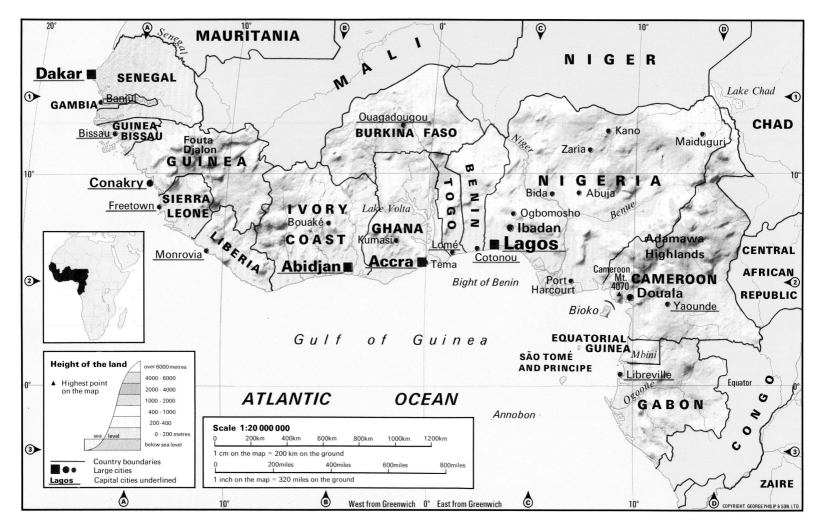

Height of the land

	over 6000 metres
	4000 - 6000
▲ Highest point on the map	2000 - 4000
	1000 - 2000
	400 - 1000
	200 - 400
sea / level	0 - 200 metres
	below sea level

■ ●● Country boundaries
Large cities
Lagos Capital cities underlined

Scale 1:20 000 000

0   200km   400km   600km   800km   1000km   1200km

1 cm on the map = 200 km on the ground

0   200miles   400miles   600miles   800miles

1 inch on the map = 320 miles on the ground

West from Greenwich   0°   East from Greenwich

COPYRIGHT. GEORGE PHILIP & SON. LTD.

There are lots of countries in West Africa. In the last 300 years, European countries grabbed parts of the coastline and later they took over the inland areas as well. Now, all the countries are independent, but still use the language of those who once ruled them. English, French, Spanish or Portuguese is spoken. Many Africans speak a European language as well as one or more African languages. Nigeria is the largest and most important country in West Africa. It has over 100 million people – more than any other African country. Although English is the official language, there are about 240 others in Nigeria!

◄**Market day.** *Red peppers for sale in Bida, Nigeria. Red peppers are very popular in West Africa – they give a strong flavour in cooking. Markets are important in both towns and villages in all the countries of West Africa. Most of the selling is done by women.*

Puzzle picture

Why is this man building all these mounds? Make a guess – then turn to page 96.

◁ **Extinct volcanoes.** *Long ago these mountains in Cameroon were volcanoes. Now only the cores of the volcanoes are left: the rest has been eroded away. Notice the thatched roofs of the houses.*

Everywhere in West Africa there is rapid progress. Most children now go to primary school, and the capital cities have televisions and airports. But many people are still very poor.

The southern part of West Africa, near the Equator, is forested. The tall trees are being felled for their hardwood. Many crops are grown in the forest area and sold overseas: cocoa (for chocolate-making in England); coffee, pineapples and bananas (for export to France); rubber (for car and lorry tyres). The main food crops are root crops, such as cassava and yams.

Further north, the trees thin out and there is savanna. The tall grass with some trees is suitable for cattle farming. There are big herds of cattle, and beautiful leather goods are on sale in the markets. Cotton and groundnuts (peanuts) are grown in the

savanna lands. The main food crops are grass-like: rice, maize, sorghum and millet.

Yeji ferry, Ghana. *This big ferry carries lorries, cars, people and their heavy loads across Lake Volta. This man-made lake flooded Ghana's main road to the north. You can see trees that died as the water rose in the new lake.* ▷

Harvesting rice in Ghana. *This view could be in Europe or North America! Huge combine-harvesters are reaping rice on a large farm in northern Ghana. But most farms are very small.* ▷

EAST AND CENTRAL AFRICA

Bus services in Africa

Bus journeys in Africa are exciting, and the fares are very cheap, but many roads are very bumpy!

'Safari' is the Swahili word for 'journey'. This bus ticket is for a journey (safari) in Tanzania from Moshi to Dar es Salaam.

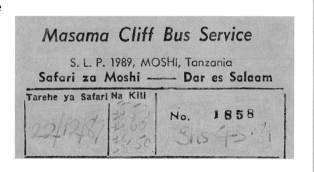

Masama Cliff Bus Service
S. L. P. 1989, MOSHI, Tanzania
Safari za Moshi ———— Dar es Salaam

Tarehe ya Safari Na Kiti

No. 1858

Fishermen, Zaïre. *Each one of these fishing boats is made from a single tree, hollowed out with an axe. They are called dug-out canoes – there is no danger of a leak in the boat!*

Central Africa is mostly lowland, with magnificent trees in the tropical rain-forest in Zaïre and Congo. Some timber is used for buildings and canoes (see photograph above left); some is exported. The cleared land can grow many tropical crops.

East Africa is mostly high savanna land with long grass, and scattered trees. Small parts are reserved for wild animals (see opposite page); in other parts, there are large farms for export crops such as coffee and tea. But in most of East Africa, the people keep cattle and grow crops for their own needs.

The Somali Republic, Djibouti, northern Kenya, and northern Ethiopia are desert areas.

Ethiopia is largely mountainous. In most years there is plenty of rain, but this can bring floods and wash away the good soil. In 1985, the country had a terrible famine.

In all these countries the population is growing fast, there is much poverty, and people are moving to the cities. But there are also many signs of development: new farm projects, new ports and roads, and new schools.

Picking tea in Nandi province, Kenya. *The tender young leaves are picked by hand and taken to a factory where they will be dried and crushed. Tea grows well in the highlands of East Africa. It is an important export of Kenya.*

The Masai people *live mainly by herding cattle on the plains near the border of Kenya and Tanzania. These teenage boys are dressed as warriors. They learn to hunt and to guard the cattle. A Masai man has been Prime Minister of Tanzania.*

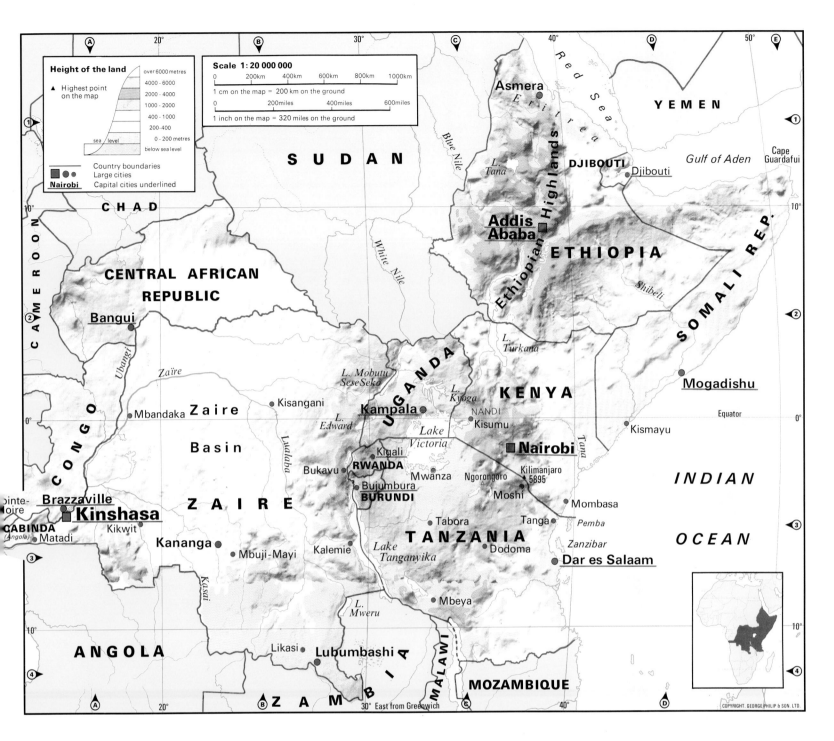

Height of the land

▲	Highest point on the map

over 6000 metres
4000 - 6000
2000 - 4000
1000 - 2000
400 - 1000
200 - 400
0 - 200 metres
sea level
below sea level

Country boundaries
Large cities
Nairobi Capital cities underlined

Scale 1: 20 000 000

| 0 | 200km | 400km | 600km | 800km | 1000km |

1 cm on the map = 200 km on the ground

| 0 | 200miles | 400miles | 600miles |

1 inch on the map = 320 miles on the ground

SUDAN

CHAD

CAMEROON

CENTRAL AFRICAN REPUBLIC

Bangui

CONGO

Brazzaville

Kinshasa

CABINDA (Angola) Matadi

Kikwit

ZAIRE

Zaïre

Mbandaka

Kisangani

Basin

Kananga

Mbuji-Mayi

Kalemie

L. Mweru

Likasi

Lubumbashi

ANGOLA

ZAMBIA

Kasai

Lualaba

Lake Tanganyika

MALAWI

MOZAMBIQUE

Asmera

Eritrea

Red Sea

YEMEN

Gulf of Aden

Cape Guardafui

DJIBOUTI

Djibouti

Addis Ababa

ETHIOPIA

Ethiopian Highlands

L. Tana

Blue Nile

White Nile

SOMALI REP.

Shibeli

L. Turkana

L. Mobutu Sese Seko

UGANDA

Kampala

L. Edward

L. Kyoga

KENYA

NANDI

Kisumu

Mogadishu

Kismayu

Equator

Lake Victoria

Kigali

RWANDA

Bukavu

Bujumbura

BURUNDI

Mwanza

Ngorongoro

Nairobi

Kilimanjaro 5895

Moshi

Mombasa

Tanga

Pemba

Tana

INDIAN OCEAN

Tabora

TANZANIA

Dodoma

Zanzibar

Dar es Salaam

Mbeya

East from Greenwich

COPYRIGHT. GEORGE PHILIP & SON. LTD.

Zebra and wildebeest *at Ngorongoro, Tanzania. People come from all over the world to go on wildlife safaris in East Africa. This lake is in the crater of an old volcano. Animals gather to drink the water, because there is no other water nearby in the long dry season.*

The game reserves of East Africa are carefully managed to conserve the wildlife. Elephants, lions, and giraffes are only 'shot' by cameras now: guns are banned. The money spent by tourists is very important for Kenya and Tanzania.

59

SOUTHERN AFRICA

Most of southern Africa is a high, flat plateau. The rivers cannot be used by ships because of big waterfalls like the Victoria Falls (see page 61). But the rivers can be useful. Two huge dams have been built on the River Zambezi – at Kariba (in Zambia) and at Cabora Bassa (in Mozambique). The map shows the lakes behind each dam. The power of the falling water is used to make electricity.

Angola and **Mozambique** used to be Portuguese colonies, and Portuguese is still their official language – though many different African languages are spoken, too. Most of the other countries shown on the map have English as their official language.

Notice that many southern African countries are land-locked: they have no coastline. The railways leading to the ports in neighbouring countries are very important. Copper from Zambia and Botswana and asbestos from Zimbabwe are sent abroad in this way.

The **Republic of South Africa** is the wealthiest country in Africa. It has the richest gold-mine in the world, and also priceless diamond-mines. But most of the black people are very poor. For many years, they were kept apart from the white people by the government, which is run by white people. This policy is called apartheid.

All the other countries of southern Africa disagree with apartheid – even Lesotho, a country which is completely surrounded by South Africa. Some parts of South Africa have been made into Bantustans – mini-countries which are partly run by Africans. But they are not recognized as real countries by the United Nations, so they are not on our map.

A village in Zambia

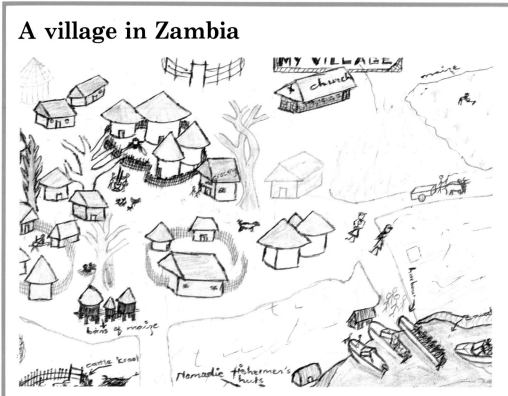

Sianga drew this picture of her village during a lesson at her school in Zambia. Her village is close to the River Zambezi in the west of the country.

An unfriendly notice *in three languages on a white-owned poultry farm in South Africa.*
▽

▲

A baobab tree. *In almost all southern Africa there is a long, hot dry season. The baobab tree is good at surviving a long drought. It has a specially fat trunk and main branches which hold water like a sponge and help to keep it alive.*

World Greats

The **Victoria Falls** (*right*) are on the River Zambezi, at the border of Zambia and Zimbabwe. Africans call the falls *Mosi-oi-tunya* – 'the smoke that thunders'. They were named after the English Queen Victoria by the explorer David Livingstone.

The world's **oldest mines** are in Swaziland. Iron ore was mined here 43,000 years ago.

The world's **deepest mine** is the gold-mine at Carletonville, South Africa. It is 3777 metres deep – and still getting deeper!

The world's **biggest diamond** was found near Pretoria, South Africa, in 1905.

Mining diamonds. *Diamonds are mined in several countries in southern Africa. The huge mine shown here* (above right) *is in*

Namibia. The desert is scraped away to reach the rock beneath, where diamonds are found. The yellow lorry is huge, but looks very small in this vast mine.

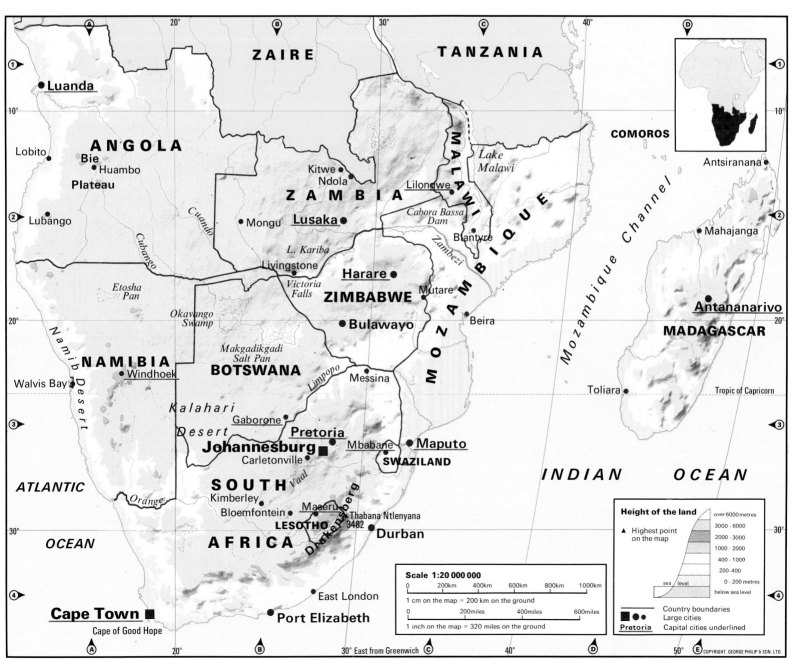

Scale 1:20 000 000

| 0 | 200km | 400km | 600km | 800km | 1000km |

1 cm on the map = 200 km on the ground

| 0 | 200miles | 400miles | 600miles |

1 inch on the map = 320 miles on the ground

Height of the land

▲ Highest point on the map

over 6000 metres
3000 - 6000
2000 - 3000
1000 - 2000
400 - 1000
200 - 400
sea level 0 - 200 metres
below sea level

Country boundaries
Large cities
Pretoria Capital cities underlined

In South Africa, Pretoria is shown as the capital but the parliament meets in Cape Town.

61

COPYRIGHT. GEORGE PHILIP & SON. LTD.

NORTH AMERICA

North America includes many Arctic islands, a huge mainland area (quite narrow in Central America) and the islands in the Caribbean Sea. The map shows the great mountain ranges which are the most impressive feature of this continent. Almost all the west is mountainous; these are mostly fold mountains but the highest peaks are volcanoes. The Appalachian Moun- tains in the east are also fold moun- tains. And the island chains of the northwest (the Aleutian Islands) and the southeast (the West Indies) are the tops of underwater ranges.

Fruit market, Barbados, West Indies. *The West Indies have hot sunshine and plenty of rain. This is an ideal climate for growing excellent fruit. Which types of fruit can you recognize in this market? (Answer on page 96.)*

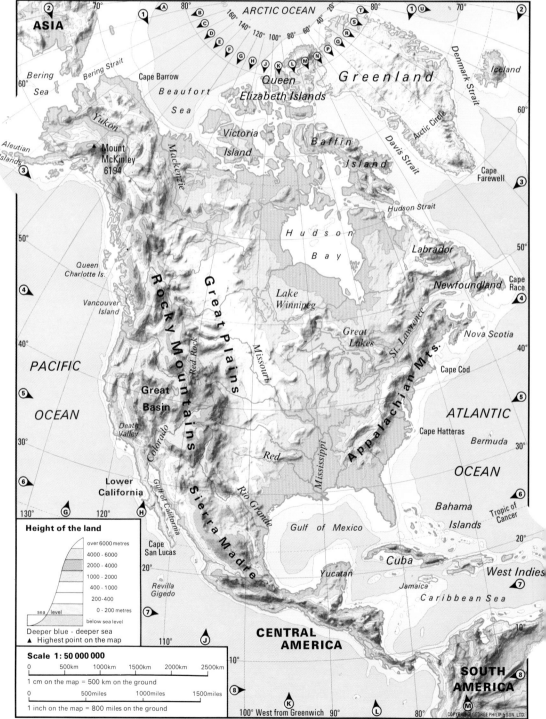

Height of the land

over 6000 metres
4000 - 6000
2000 - 4000
1000 - 2000
400 - 1000
200 - 400
sea level 0 - 200 metres
below sea level
Deeper blue - deeper sea
▲ Highest point on the map

Scale 1: 50 000 000

| 0 | 500km | 1000km | 1500km | 2000km | 2500km |

1 cm on the map = 500 km on the ground

| 0 | 500miles | 1000miles | 1500miles |

1 inch on the map = 800 miles on the ground

The political map of North America is quite a simple one. The boundary between Canada and the USA is mostly at exactly 49°N. Four of the five Great Lakes have one shore in Canada and one shore in the USA.* Canada's two biggest cities, Toronto and Montreal, are south of the 49° line! Find them on the map on page 65.

The eight countries of Central America have more complicated boundaries. Six of these countries have two coastlines. The map shows that one country has a coastline only on the Pacific Ocean, and one has a coastline only on the Caribbean Sea.* The West Indies are made up of islands and there are lots of countries too. They are shown in more detail on pages 74 and 75.

Greenland was a colony of Denmark until quite recently, but now it is self-governing. Most of Greenland is covered by ice all year.

*Which ones? Answers on page 96.

Find them on the map on page 65.

They are shown in more detail on pages 74 and 75.

*Which ones? Answers on page 96.

Fact box: North America

Area 24,249,000 square kilometres

Highest point Mount McKinley (Alaska), 6194 metres

Lowest point Death Valley (California), 86 metres below sea-level

Longest river Red Rock-Missouri-Mississippi, 5970 kilometres

Largest lake Lake Superior*, 82,350 square kilometres

Biggest country Canada, 9,976,140 square kilometres

Smallest country Grenada (West Indies), 344 square kilometres

Richest country USA

Poorest country Haiti

Most crowded country Barbados

Least crowded country Canada

*The world's largest *fresh-water* lake

Flyovers, Los Angeles, USA.
There are four levels of road at this road junction in Los Angeles, yet there is a traffic-jam as well! The USA has more cars than any other country.

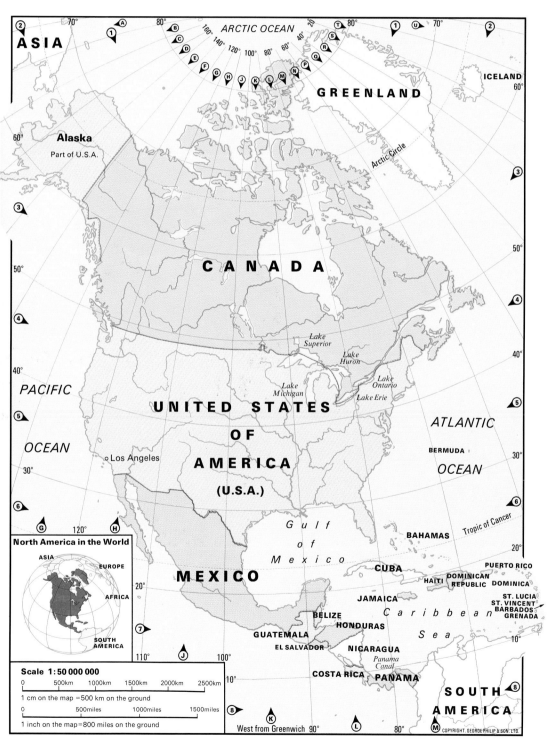

North America in the World

Scale 1:50 000 000

1 cm on the map = 500 km on the ground

1 inch on the map = 800 miles on the ground

CANADA

Coin and flag. *Both the 1 cent coin and the flag show the national emblem of Canada, the maple leaf. In summer, the leaves of the maple tree are green, but in the fall (autumn) the leaves turn bright red. Canada's woodlands are specially beautiful in September and October (see photograph below right).*

Canadian Contrasts

This stamp is an air-picture of the prairies of central Canada. The huge flat fields of grain reach to the far horizon, and beyond. The only big buildings are grain elevators, for storing the harvested wheat.

In western Canada, the Rocky Mountains are high and jagged. There are glaciers among the peaks.

Only one country in the world is bigger than Canada*, but thirty countries have more people than Canada. Most of Canada is almost empty: very few people live on the islands of the north, or in the Northwest Territories, or in the western mountains, or near Hudson Bay. The farmland of the prairies (see the stamp) is uncrowded too. So . . . where *do* Canadians live?

The answer is that more Canadians live in cities than in the countryside. The map shows where the biggest cities are – all of them are in the southern part of Canada, and none are as far north as Norway or Sweden in Europe.

The photographs and stamps show Canada in summer. In winter, it is very cold indeed in central and northern Canada. Children go to school even when it is 40° below zero.

*Which country? See pages 38–9.

The Niagara Falls *are between Lake Erie and Lake Ontario, on the border of the USA and Canada. The tourists on the boat may get soaked by the spray! Big ships have to use a canal, with locks, to get past the falls.*

Languages in Canada
Canada has two official languages: French and English. So the stamps say 'Postes/Postage', instead of only 'Postage'. Most French-speaking Canadians live in the province of Quebec.

The biggest city in Quebec is Montreal: it is four times as big as Ottawa, the capital of Canada.

A long-distance train, *with diesel engines and silver coaches, crosses a viaduct in the province of Ontario. It is 4590 kilometres from Montreal to Vancouver by train. A hundred years ago it was the trans-Canada railway that helped to unite Canada as one country.*

How to remember the five Great Lakes
Try using the first letters of the Great Lakes to make a sentence:

Superior	Super
Michigan	Man
Huron	Helps
Erie	Every
Ontario	One

Now you'll *never* forget the west-to-east order of the Great Lakes!

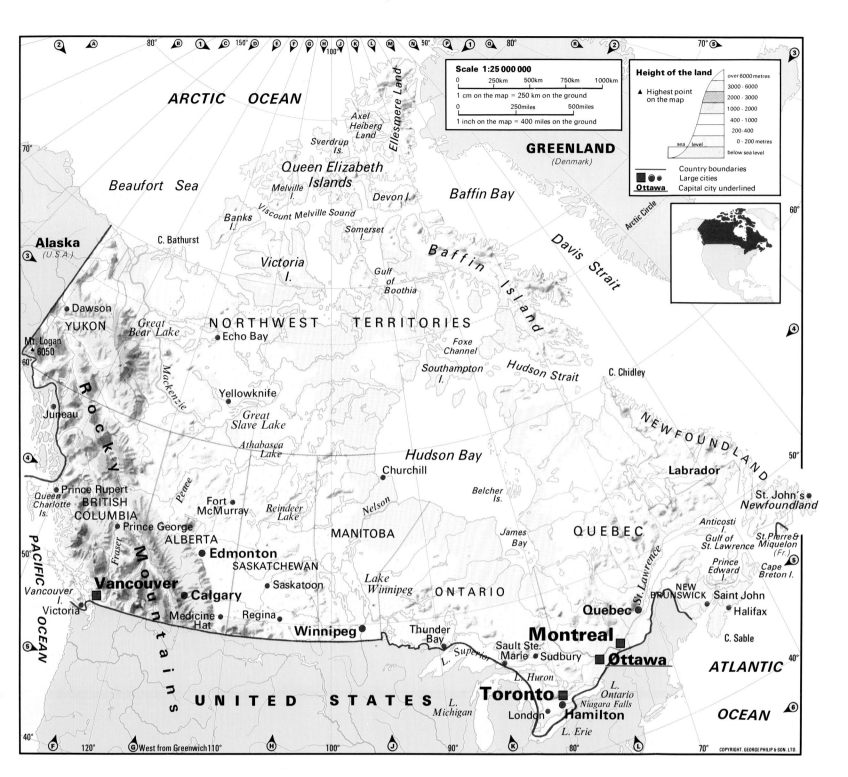

ARCTIC OCEAN

Axel
Heiberg
Land

Sverdrup
Is.

Queen Elizabeth
Islands

Melville
I.

Devon I.

Baffin Bay

GREENLAND
(Denmark)

Banks
I.

Viscount Melville Sound

Somerset
I.

Davis Strait

Beaufort Sea

C. Bathurst

Victoria
I.

Gulf
of
Boothia

Baffin Island

Arctic Circle

Alaska
(U.S.A.)

Dawson

YUKON

Great
Bear Lake

NORTHWEST   TERRITORIES

Echo Bay

Foxe
Channel

Mt. Logan
▲ 6050

Mackenzie

Juneau

Yellowknife

Great
Slave Lake

Southampton
I.

Hudson Strait

C. Chidley

Rocky

Athabasca
Lake

Hudson Bay

Churchill

NEWFOUNDLAND

Labrador

Queen
Charlotte
Is.

Prince Rupert

BRITISH
COLUMBIA

Peace

Fort
McMurray

Reindeer
Lake

Nelson

Belcher
Is.

St. John's
Newfoundland

Prince George

Fraser

ALBERTA

Edmonton

SASKATCHEWAN

James
Bay

QUEBEC

Anticosti
I.

Gulf of
St. Lawrence

St. Pierre &
Miquelon
(Fr.)

PACIFIC

Mountains

Vancouver

Calgary

Saskatoon

Lake
Winnipeg

ONTARIO

Prince
Edward
I.

Cape
Breton I.

Vancouver I.
Victoria

Medicine
Hat

Regina

St. Lawrence

NEW
BRUNSWICK

Saint John

OCEAN

Winnipeg

Thunder
Bay

Quebec

Halifax

C. Sable

Sault Ste.
Marie · Sudbury

Montreal

UNITED   STATES

L. Superior

Ottawa

ATLANTIC

L.
Michigan

L. Huron

Toronto

L.
Ontario

Niagara Falls

OCEAN

London

Hamilton

L. Erie

West from Greenwich 110°

COPYRIGHT. GEORGE PHILIP & SON. LTD.

Scale 1:25 000 000

0   250km   500km   750km   1000km

1 cm on the map = 250 km on the ground

0   250miles   500miles

1 inch on the map = 400 miles on the ground

Height of the land

▲ Highest point
on the map

over 6000 metres
3000 - 6000
2000 - 3000
1000 - 2000
400 - 1000
200 - 400
0 - 200 metres
below sea level

sea level

Country boundaries

Large cities

Ottawa   Capital city underlined

◁ **Montreal: old and new.** *The old houses have been pulled down, to make way for huge new office blocks. Three million people live in Montreal.*

The St Lawrence. *This big ship is passing islands in the St Lawrence river. The ship is going from the Great Lakes to the Atlantic Ocean. A seaway with huge locks has been built to bypass the rapids, shallows and waterfalls on parts of the river.* ▷

USA

Juneau is the capital of Alaska, see page 65.

Alaska is the biggest state of the USA – but it has the fewest people. It was bought from Russia in 1867 for seven million dollars: the best bargain ever, particularly as oil was discovered a hundred years later. Oil has helped Alaska to become rich. Fish and

timber are the other main products. Much of Alaska is mountainous or covered in forest. In the north, there is darkness all day in December, and months of ice-cold weather.

Flag of Alaska. *The flag of Alaska shows stars in the northern sky known as the 'plough' or 'the big dipper'. At the top right is the Pole Star: this reminds us that Alaska is in the far north. The flag was chosen in a competition; the winner was only 13 years old.*

These are 48 of the 50 states. The other two are Alaska (map above) and Hawaii (map below).
⭐ State capital

ABBREVIATIONS
VT. = Vermont
N.H. = New Hampshire
MASS. = Massachusetts
CONN. = Connecticut
D.C. = District of Columbia

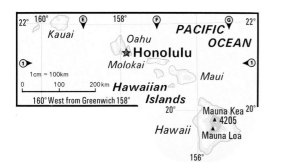

Hawaii *is the newest state in the USA: it became a state in 1959. Honolulu is on Oahu island.*

These faraway Pacific islands are the tops of volcanoes, over 3000

kilometres from mainland USA (see the map on page 83). If the height of Mauna Kea is measured from the sea-bed, it is 10,023 metres, the tallest mountain in the world.

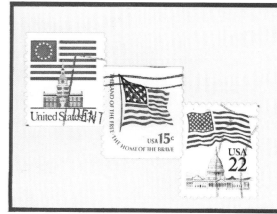

Stars and stripes

In 1776 there were only 13 states in the USA; so the US flag had 13 stars and 13 stripes. As more and more states joined the USA, more stars were added to the flag. Now there are 50 states, and 50 stars. But the 13 stripes on today's flag still recall the original 13 states.

The maps show the 50 states of the USA. The first 13 states were all on the east coast: these states were settled by Europeans who had sailed across the Atlantic (see the photograph of a pilgrim ship on page 69).

As the Americans moved westward, so more and more states were formed. The western states are bigger than the states in the east. You can see their straight boundaries on the map.

Who are 'the Americans'?

Out of every 100 people in the USA, 83 have ancestors from Europe. Colonists came from Britain to the eastern states, from France to the southern states, and from Spain to the Pacific coastline in the west. Later on,

people came from almost all parts of Europe to the USA. About 12 people out of every 100 came from West Africa, brought to the USA as slaves to work in the southern states. By 1865, the slaves were free. Many black Americans now live in the northeast USA. More recently, many Spanish-speaking people have entered the USA from Mexico and from Puerto Rico in the Caribbean.

There are fewer than one million American Indians now, some of whom live on special 'reservations'.

5 cent coin. *E PLURIBUS UNUM on this coin is Latin for 'Out of many – one': many peoples have come together to become one country. This 5 cent piece is called a nickel.*

State flags. *Each state has its own flag and some of them tell you about the history of the state.*

Wyoming *has a buffalo in the centre of its flag because this state was part of the Wild West where buffaloes used to roam freely.*

Mississippi *has the French flag (red, white and blue stripes) because it belonged to France until 1803.*

The cross at top left was used as a flag by the southern states in the Civil War in 1861–5.

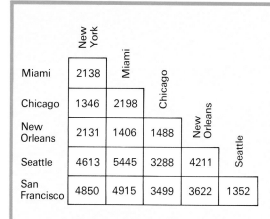

American football. *The Washington Redskins play the San Francisco 49ers. The team from the west coast has travelled 4500 kilometres for this game. The players travel by air – it takes three days to cross the USA by train!*

	New York	Miami	Chicago	New Orleans	Seattle
Miami	2138				
Chicago	1346	2198			
New Orleans	2131	1406	1488		
Seattle	4613	5445	3288	4211	
San Francisco	4850	4915	3499	3622	1352

Road distances in kilometres

Distance chart

Read the chart just like a tables-chart, or a graph. The distance chart shows how big the USA is. In fact, New York is nearer to London, England, than it is to San Francisco! How far is it from Seattle to Miami? New Orleans to Chicago? (Find these places on the maps on pages 68–71). (Answers on page 96.)

EASTERN USA

Which US city is most important?

Washington is the capital city, where the President lives. But *New York* has far more people and industries than Washington. So *both* are the most important city – but in different ways.

The map shows only half the USA, but over three-quarters of the population live in this half of the country.

The great cities of the northeast were the first big industrial areas in America. Pittsburgh's American football team is still called the Pittsburgh Steelers, even though many of the steel-works have closed down.

In recent years, many people have moved from the 'snow-belt' of the north to the 'sun-belt' of the south. New industries are booming in the south, where once there was much poverty. And many older people retire to Florida, where even midwinter feels almost like summer.

The Appalachian Mountains are beautiful, especially in the fall (autumn), when the leaves of the trees turn red. But this area is the poorest part of the USA. Coal-mines have closed and farmland is poor. The good farmland is west of the Appalachians, where you can drive for hundreds of kilometres past wheat and sweetcorn. In the south it is hot enough for cotton, tobacco and peanuts to be successful crops.

Washington, DC. *There is a world of difference between the well-kept rich suburbs* (above) *and the run-down slum area* (right) *of Washington, DC, the capital city of the USA.*

Plan for better cities!

Turn the book clockwise and you will see patios, parks and gardens among the skyscrapers!

Manhattan Island, New York. *The world's first skyscrapers were built on Manhattan Island: the hard granite rock gave good foundations. The older skyscrapers each have a different shape; the newer ones are flat-topped.*

Plantation-owner's house in Virginia. *Plantation owners grew rich from tobacco and cotton. They lived in fine houses like this one. But their slaves lived in very poor houses.*

Winter in Pittsburgh. *Winter in the northern USA can be very cold indeed. But these Pittsburgh children are enjoying the fresh, crisp snow, before it becomes polluted by smoke from the steel-works and factories.*

The Earth from the Moon

This is the view that American astronauts saw from the Moon. Half the Earth is in darkness. Neil Armstrong of the USA was the first man on the Moon, 21 July 1969.

Pilgrim ship, New England. *The Pilgrim Fathers sailed to America in 1620 from England to start a new life. In 1957 a replica pilgrim ship was built and sailed to America.*

Puzzle stamp

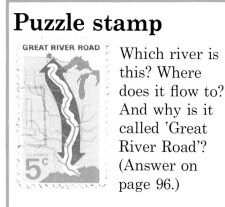

Which river is this? Where does it flow to? And why is it called 'Great River Road'? (Answer on page 96.)

Scale 1:20 000 000

| 0 | 200km | 400km | 600km | 800km |

1 cm on the map = 200 km on the ground

| 0 | 200miles | 400miles |

1 inch on the map = 320 miles on the ground

Height of the land

- over 6000 metres
- 4000 - 6000
- 2000 - 4000
- 1000 - 2000
- 400 - 1000
- 200-400
- 0 - 200 metres
- below sea level

▲ Highest point on the map

Country boundaries
●● Large cities
Washington Capital city underlined
For the states of the U.S.A. see page 66

CANADA

Fargo
Duluth
Lake Superior
St. Paul
Minneapolis
Sioux Falls
Milwaukee
Detroit
Chicago
Toledo
Cleveland
Omaha
Missouri
Indianapolis
Columbus
Pittsburgh
Kansas City
Cincinnati
Ohio
St. Louis
Wichita
Louisville
Richmond
Tulsa
Nashville
Mt. Mitchell 2037
Charlotte
Oklahoma City
Arkansas
Memphis
Tennessee
Chattanooga
Atlanta
Birmingham
Charleston
Fort Worth
Dallas
Montgomery
Austin
Baton Rouge
Jacksonville
Houston
New Orleans
San Antonio
Tampa
Palm Beach
Everglades
Gulf of Mexico
Miami
C. Canaveral
C. Sable
Key West
West from Greenwich

Boston
Albany
Hudson
C. Cod
Buffalo
Providence
New York
Philadelphia
Baltimore
Washington
Norfolk
ATLANTIC
OCEAN
BAHAMAS

COPYRIGHT. GEORGE PHILIP & SON. LTD.

WESTERN USA

Grand Canyon, Arizona.
The Colorado river has cut a huge canyon a mile deep in this desert area of the USA. The mountains slowly rose, while the river kept digging its valley deeper.

Wheat harvest, USA. *Three huge combine harvesters move across a field of wheat. 150 years ago, this land was covered in grass and grazed by buffaloes. Much of this wheat will go abroad.*

American football

Many of the team names have a meaning that is linked to their city's geography or history.

San Francisco 49ers 1849 was the year of the great Californian Gold Rush, when many people came to look for gold.

Denver Broncos Denver, Colorado, was a centre for cowboys in the days of the Wild West: 'bucking broncos' were their horses!

Houston Oilers Houston, Texas, became a very wealthy city after oil was discovered.

Seattle Seahawks Seattle, Washington State, is on an inlet of the Pacific Ocean.

Do you know any other teams?

Rodeo in Montana. *There are few real cowboys nowadays – and trucks are used more than horses. But rodeos are popular with local people – and with tourists. At this junior rodeo at Big Timber, Montana, a young rider is trying to show his skill.*

California

California now has more people in it than any other state in the USA. It has every advantage. In the Central Valley the climate is right for many crops: oranges from California are well-known in the USA and abroad. Grapes grow well, and are made into wine.

The desert of the south is attractive to retired people – many people migrate here from all over the USA.

Many areas on this map have hardly any people. The Rocky Mountains are beautiful for holidays, but it is hard to make a living there. The only big city on the high plateaus west of the Rockies is Salt Lake City, Utah. Some former mining towns are now 'ghost towns': when the mines closed, all the people left. The toughest area of all is the desert land of Arizona in the southwest. The mountains and deserts were a great problem to the pioneers.

East of the Rockies are the Great Plains. The dry plains have enormous cattle ranches; where there is enough rain, crops of wheat and sweetcorn (maize) stretch to the horizon.

The Pacific coastlands of the northwest have plenty of rain and forestry is important. The climate is quite like northwest Europe.

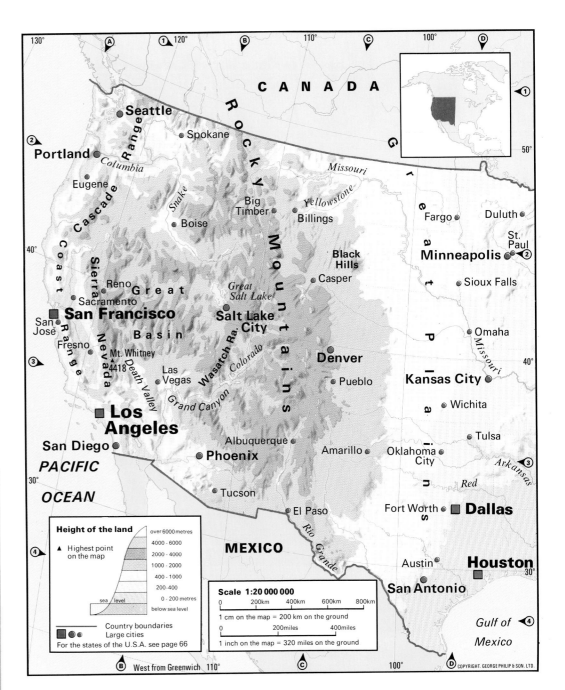

What do the names mean?

The Spanish were the first settlers in the western USA, and they have left us many Spanish names. Here are some:

Amarillo (Texas) ..Yellow
Colorado ....Coloured
El Paso
  (Texas)................The pass
Los Angeles ....The angels
Las Vegas ....The fertile
  (Nevada)   plains
San José...............St Joseph
San Francisco .....St Francis
Sierra Nevada .....Snowy
                      Mountains

Street-car, San Francisco.
Street-cars still climb the steep hills in San Francisco, California. A moving cable runs beneath the street. The car is fixed to the cable and starts with a jerk! There is a modern 'rapid transit' railway system too – but tourists prefer to see the city from the street-cars.

CENTRAL AMERICA

◁ **Ruins at Chichen Itza, Mexico.**
Great temples were built by the people known as Mayas over a thousand years ago. These amazing ruins are in Yucatan, the most easterly part of Mexico. Today, this is an area of jungle, with few people.

MEXICAN TORTILLAS

A recipe for you to cook

Ingredients
225 grams of maize flour (sweetcorn flour)
salt
water

Method
1 Mix the maize flour, salt, and water into a soft dough.
2 Pat into round shapes about $\frac{1}{2}$ centimetre thick, and 12 centimetres across.
3 Melt a little margarine in a frying-pan.
4 Place the tortillas in the hot frying-pan.
5 For best results, turn the tortillas over.
6 Serve at once!

You have now cooked one of the most important meals of Central America. Maize (sweetcorn) was developed as a crop in the Americas, and is now grown in many parts of the world. You eat maize often as Corn Flakes and semolina.

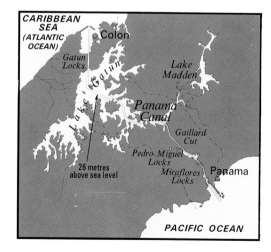

CARIBBEAN SEA (ATLANTIC OCEAN)
Colon
Gatun Locks
Lake Madden
Lake Gatun
Panama Canal
Gaillard Cut
Pedro Miguel Locks
Miraflores Locks
Panama
26 metres above sea level
PACIFIC OCEAN

The Panama Canal *links the Caribbean Sea with the Pacific Ocean. It was opened in 1914. Many workers died of fever while digging the canal through the jungle. It is 82 kilometres long, and the deepest cutting is 82 metres deep – the world's biggest 'ditch'!*
There are six locks along the route of the canal. The photograph (below left) shows three ships in Gatun Lake, 26 metres above sea-level (see map). Over 15,000 ships use the canal each year, and sometimes there are 'traffic jams' at the locks: it is the busiest big ship canal in the world. Before the Panama Canal was built, the only sea route from Pacific to Atlantic was round South America. ◁

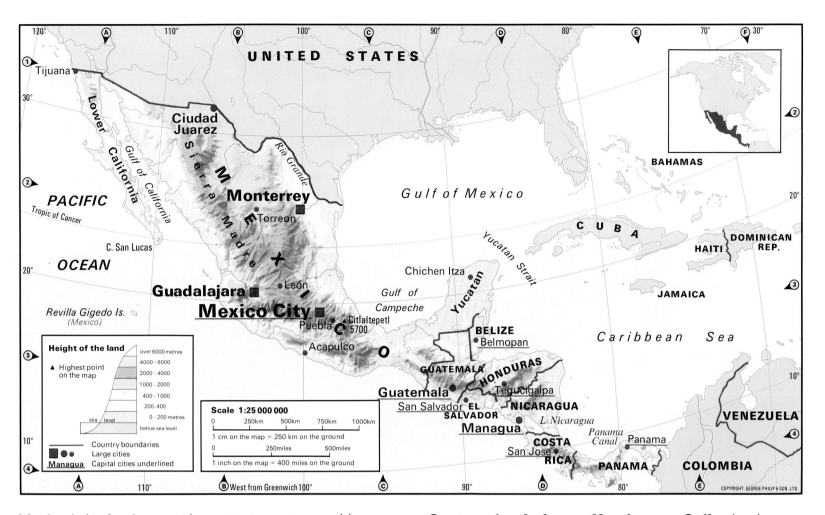

Mexico is by far the most important country on this map. Over 82 million people live in Mexico – more than in any country in Europe. Mexico City has a population of about 15 million: it is one of the biggest cities in the world. A major earthquake did much damage there in 1985.

Most Mexicans live on the high plateau of central Mexico. There are very few people in the northern desert, in Lower California in the northwest, in the southern jungle, or in Yucatan in the east.

The other seven countries on this map are quite small. None of them has as many people as Mexico City!

Once ruled by Spain, these countries have been independent since the 1820s. Revolutions and civil wars have caused many problems in Central America. But the climate is good for growing many tropical crops – once the jungle has been cleared.

What do the names mean?

Many names in the countries of Central America are based on Spanish, the official language.

El Salvador The Saviour (Jesus Christ)
San José (capital of Costa Rica) St Joseph
Costa Rica The rich coast
Pacific Ocean Peaceful ocean

Guatemala: drying coffee-beans. *Coffee berries grow on bushes in tropical countries. The berries are picked, and the seeds taken out and dried in the sun. We call these dried seeds coffee-beans.*

The man in the photograph is turning the beans, so that they dry on both sides.

Coffee is the most important export of several Central American countries. Many other tropical crops are exported, including sugar, bananas and pineapple.

WEST INDIES

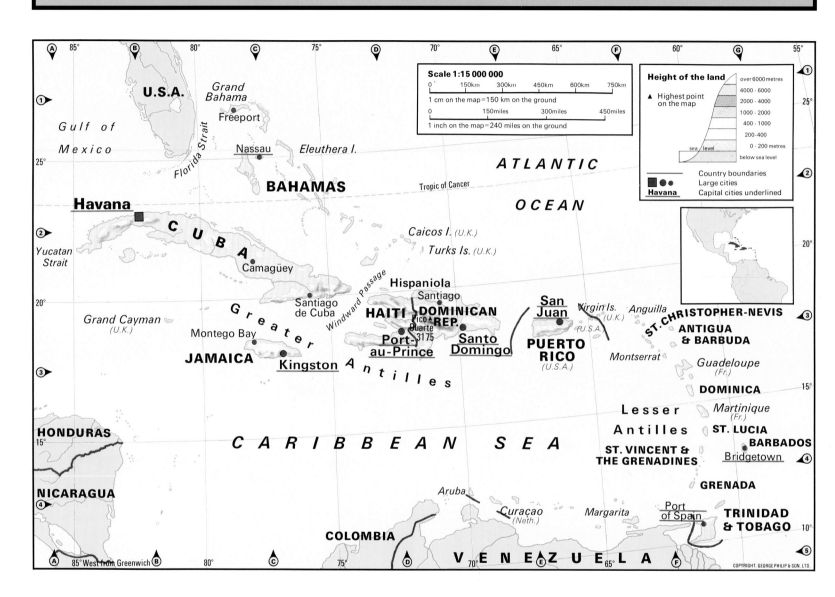

Scale 1:15 000 000					
0	150km	300km	450km	600km	750km

1 cm on the map = 150 km on the ground

0	150miles	300miles	450miles

1 inch on the map = 240 miles on the ground

Height of the land

▲ Highest point on the map

	over 6000 metres
	4000 - 6000
	2000 - 4000
	1000 - 2000
	400 - 1000
	200 - 400
	0 - 200 metres
sea level	
	below sea level

— Country boundaries
● Large cities
Havana ◯ Capital cities underlined

Farming in Jamaica

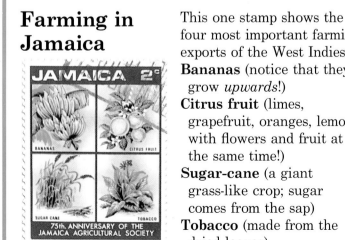

This one stamp shows the four most important farming exports of the West Indies.

Bananas (notice that they grow *upwards*!)

Citrus fruit (limes, grapefruit, oranges, lemons; with flowers and fruit at the same time!)

Sugar-cane (a giant grass-like crop; sugar comes from the sap)

Tobacco (made from the dried leaves)

The West Indies are a large group of islands in the Caribbean Sea. Some islands are high and volcanic, others are low coral islands – but all of them are beautiful. Most West Indians have African ancestors: they were brought from West Africa as slaves, to work in the sugar and tobacco fields.

Today, most of the islands are independent countries – and tourism is more important than farming in many places. Winter is the best time to visit; summer is very hot and humid, with the risk of hurricanes. In recent years many West Indians have emigrated to the UK from Commonwealth islands, to France from Guadeloupe and Martinique, and to the USA from Puerto Rico. A few islands have developed their minerals, for example bauxite in Jamaica and oil in Trinidad.

Coconut-palms and beach, Barbados. *It is beautiful – but beware! The tropical sun can quickly burn your skin. And if you seek shade under the coconut-palms, you might get hit by a big coconut! Even so, the West Indies are very popular with tourists – especially Americans escaping from cold winters.*

Loading bananas, Dominica. *Bananas are the main export of several islands. Here women are carrying heavy loads of bananas on their heads to the small boats which take the bananas to the Geest banana ship. The bananas travel to Europe in this refrigerated ship. Loading the ship is easier where islands have deep-water harbours.*

Dutch colonial houses, Curaçao. *The island of Curaçao has been Dutch for many years. The colonists came from the Netherlands, and tried to build houses just like the ones at home. Several other small West Indian islands still have European connections.*

West Indian variety

In **Cuba**, Spanish is the main language. But Cuba is allied with the USSR, not with Spain: it has a communist government.

St Vincent is part of the Commonwealth and seems very British (but arrowroot and breadfruit only grow in the tropics).

Guadeloupe is not just French – it is officially part of France. This stamp was used in Guadeloupe *and* in all of France!

Curaçao is Dutch: the stamp shows Dutch colonial houses, and the Queen of the Netherlands. Compare the photograph (*right*).

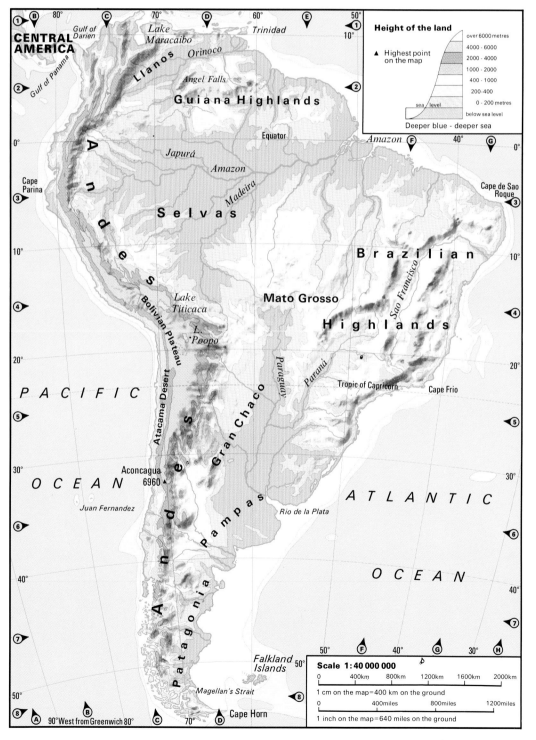

◁ **Brasilia, Brazil.** *Brasilia became the new capital of Brazil in 1960. The photograph shows the parliament building on the left, built in concrete and shaped like a bowl, and a tall office block. Most Brazilians live near the coast, and Brasilia was a brave attempt to get people to move inland: it is 1000 kilometres from the sea. Over a million people now live there.*

Height of the land

▲ Highest point on the map

	over 6000 metres
	4000 - 6000
	2000 - 4000
	1000 - 2000
	400 - 1000
	200 - 400
sea level	0 - 200 metres
	below sea level

Deeper blue - deeper sea

Scale 1 : 40 000 000

0   400km   800km   1200km   1600km   2000km

1 cm on the map = 400 km on the ground

0   400miles   800miles   1200miles

1 inch on the map = 640 miles on the ground

Fact box: South America

Area 17,600,000 square kilometres

Highest point Mount Aconcagua (Argentina), 6960 metres

Lowest point No land below sea-level

Longest river Amazon, 6448 kilometres

Largest lake Lake Titicaca (Bolivia and Peru), 8285 square kilometres

Biggest country Brazil, 8,511,965 square kilometres

Smallest country Surinam*, 163,265 square kilometres

Richest country Venezuela

Poorest country Bolivia

Most crowded country Ecuador

Least crowded country Surinam

*French Guiana is smaller, but it is not independent

◁ **Reed-boat on Lake Titicaca.**
Lake Titicaca is the highest navigable lake in the world: 3811 metres above sea-level. The fishing-boat is made of totora reeds which grow around the shores. Bundles of reeds are tied together, and even the sails are made of woven reeds.

The lake is shared between Peru and Bolivia. A steam-powered ferry-boat travels the length of the lake. A river flows southwards from Lake Titicaca to Lake Poopo, and then flows onwards and vanishes in the high, dry plateau.

Why is Lake Titicaca the only stretch of water available to the Bolivian navy? (Check the map.)

A tour of South America would be very exciting. At the Equator are the hot steamy jungles of the Amazon lowlands. To the west comes the great climb up to the Andes mountains. The peaks are so high that even the volcanoes are snow-capped all year. Travellers on buses and trains are offered extra oxygen to breathe, because the air is so thin.

Squeezed between the Andes and the Pacific Ocean in Peru and northern Chile is the world's driest desert. Further south in Chile are more wet forests – but these forests are cool. The Chilean pine (monkey-puzzle tree) originates here. But eastwards, in Argentina, there is less rain and more grass. Cattle on the Pampas are rounded up by cowboys, and further south is the very cold and dry area called Patagonia.

South America stretches further south than any other continent (apart from Antarctica). The cold and stormy tip of South America, Cape Horn, is only 1000 kilometres from Antarctica.

In every South American country, the population is growing fast. Most of the farmland is owned by a few rich people, and many people are desperately poor. Young people are leaving the countryside for the cities, most of which are encircled by shanty towns.

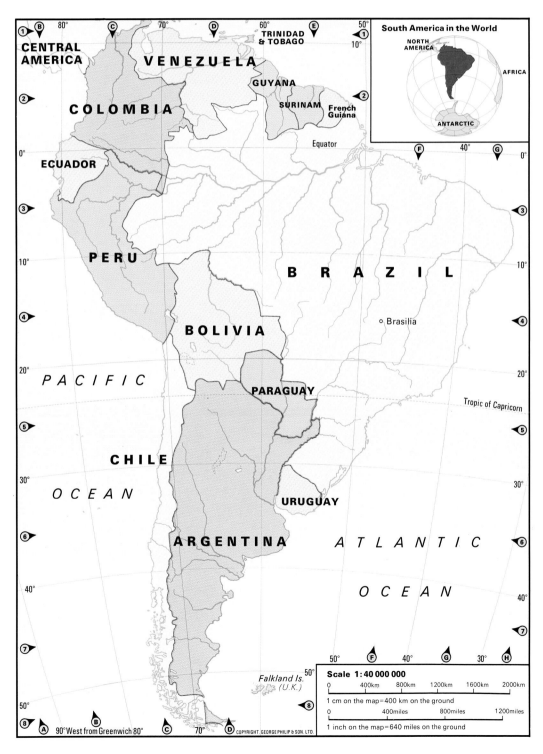

South America in the World

NORTH AMERICA

AFRICA

ANTARCTIC

Scale 1 : 40 000 000

| 0 | 400km | 800km | 1200km | 1600km | 2000km |

1 cm on the map = 400 km on the ground

| 0 | 400miles | 800miles | 1200miles |

1 inch on the map = 640 miles on the ground

COPYRIGHT GEORGE PHILIP & SON. LTD.

90° West from Greenwich 80°

TROPICAL SOUTH AMERICA

Amazon jungle *at the border of Guyana and Brazil. The hot, wet jungle covers thousands of kilometres. There is no cool season, and the forest is always green. The trees can be 50 metres high. New roads and villages, mines and dams are being built in the Brazilian jungle.*

The Andean states. Colombia, Ecuador, Peru and Bolivia are known as the Andean states. **Colombia** is known for its coffee. Bananas and other tropical crops grow near the coast of **Ecuador**, but the capital city is high in the mountains. **Peru** relies on mountain rivers to bring water to the dry coastal area.

Bolivia has the highest capital city in the world. It is the poorest country in South America: farming is difficult and even the tin-mines hardly make a profit.

East of the Andes, settlers are clearing parts of the forest.

Machu Picchu, Peru, *the lost city of the Incas, is perched on a mountainside 2400 metres above sea-level. The last Inca emperor probably lived here in 1580. The ruins were rediscovered in 1911.*

Brazil – the giant. Brazil is by far the biggest country in South America, and has more people than the rest of South America put together (about 150 million).

Most people still live near the coast. Parts of the Amazon forest are now being settled, but large areas inland are still almost empty. The poorest parts are in the northeast, where the rains often fail, and in the shanty towns around the big cities. Modern industry is growing very fast, but there are still too few jobs. Brazil has pioneered fuel made from sugar-cane for cars and trucks.

The llama *is the most important animal in the Andes – it provides milk, meat and leather for these Quechua Indian women. They are following one of the Inca tracks which linked the ancient cities.*

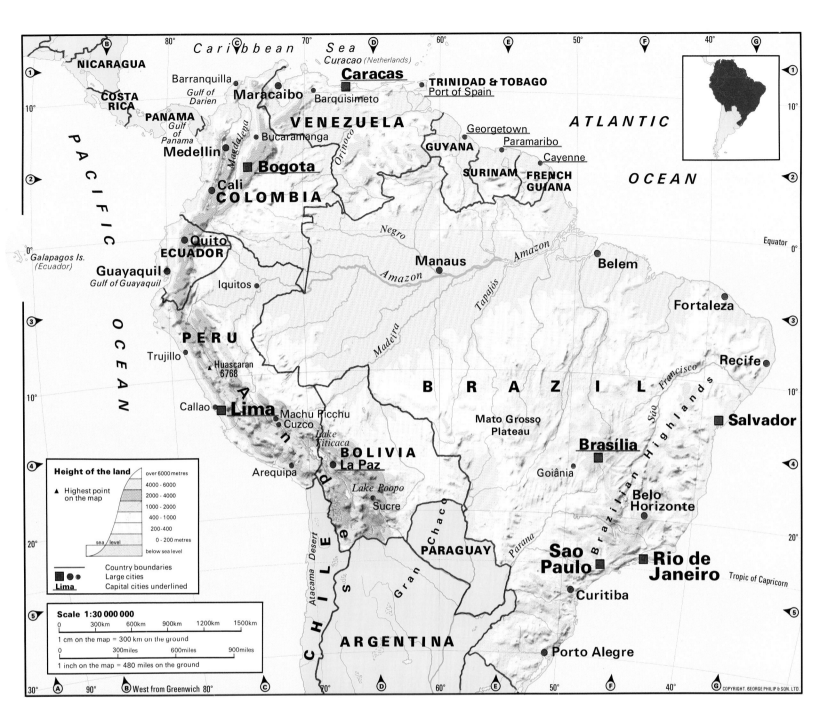

C a r i b b e a n   S e a
Curacao (Netherlands)
ATLANTIC
OCEAN

NICARAGUA
COSTA RICA
PANAMA
Gulf of Panama
Gulf of Darien
Barranquilla
Maracaibo
Medellin
Bogota
Cali
COLOMBIA
Caracas
Barquisimeto
VENEZUELA
Bucaramanga
TRINIDAD & TOBAGO
Port of Spain
Georgetown
Paramaribo
Cayenne
GUYANA
SURINAM
FRENCH GUIANA
Orinoco
Negro
Amazon
Amazon
Manaus
Belem
Fortaleza
Equator
Galapagos Is. (Ecuador)
Quito
ECUADOR
Guayaquil
Gulf of Guayaquil
Iquitos
Tapajós
Madeira
Recife
P E R U
Trujillo
▲Huascaran 6768
São Francisco
B R A Z I L
Mato Grosso Plateau
Brazilian Highlands
Salvador
Callao
Lima
Machu Picchu
Cuzco
Lake Titicaca
B O L I V I A
La Paz
Arequipa
Lake Poopo
Sucre
Brasília
Goiânia
Belo Horizonte
Gran Chaco
PARAGUAY
Parana
Sao Paulo
Rio de Janeiro
Curitiba
Tropic of Capricorn
Atacama Desert
C H I L E
A R G E N T I N A
Porto Alegre

PACIFIC OCEAN

Height of the land
▲ Highest point on the map
over 6000 metres
4000 - 6000
2000 - 4000
1000 - 2000
400 - 1000
200 - 400
0 - 200 metres
sea level
below sea level
Country boundaries
Large cities
Capital cities underlined
Lima

Scale 1:30 000 000
0   300km   600km   900km   1200km   1500km
1 cm on the map = 300 km on the ground
0   300miles   600miles   900miles
1 inch on the map = 480 miles on the ground

West from Greenwich
COPYRIGHT. GEORGE PHILIP & SON. LTD.

Cattle and cowboys. *To the south of the Amazon jungle, there is a large area of dry woodland and grassland in Brazil called the Mato Grosso. Cattle are grazed here, and horses are still used to round them up.*

Did you know?

Ecuador means *Equator*: the Equator (0°) crosses the country.

Colombia is named after Christopher *Columbus*, who sailed from Europe to the Americas in 1492.

Bolivia is named after Simon *Bolivar*, a hero of the country's war of independence in the 1820s.

La Paz, the biggest town in Bolivia, means *peace*. But there have been over 100 revolutions in Bolivia, the highest total in the world!

79

TEMPERATE SOUTH AMERICA

Chile is 4300 kilometres long, but only about 200 kilometres wide, because it is sandwiched between the Andes and the Pacific. In the *north* is the Atacama desert, the driest in the world. In one place, there was no rain for 400 years! Fortunately, rivers from the Andes permit some irrigation. Chilean nitrates come from this area. Nitrates are salts in dried-up lakes; they are used to make fertilizers and explosives.

In the *centre*, the climate is like the Mediterranean area and California, with hot dry summers and warm wet winters with westerly winds (six words begin with W: it's easy to remember!) This is a lovely climate, and most Chileans live in this area.

In the *south*, Chile is wet, windy and cool. Thick forests which include the Chilean pine (monkey-puzzle tree) cover the steep hills. The reason for these contrasts is the wind. Winds bringing cloud and rain blow from the Pacific Ocean all year in the south; but only in winter in the centre; and not at all in the north.

Geysers in the Andes, Chile. *Hot steam hisses into the cold air, 4000 metres above sea-level in the Andes of northern Chile.*

The Falkland Islands

These islands are a British colony in the South Atlantic. They are about 480 kilometres east of Argentina, which claims them as the Islas Malvinas. Britain fought an Argentine invasion in 1982, and the military force is now as large as the population (only 2000). Sheep-farming is the main occupation.

The capital city, Port Stanley, has houses that look quite like English houses, but the remote farmhouses get their post by 'mail drop' from a Beaver aircraft (see stamp above). Until recently, there were no roads to these farms. This stamp shows Argentina's claim that the Falkland Islands are part of Argentina.

The Andes

The Andes are over 7000 kilometres long, so they are the longest mountain range in the world. They are fold mountains, with a very steep western side, and a gentler eastern side. Most of the high peaks are volcanoes: they are the highest volcanoes in the world. Mount Aconcagua (6960 metres) is an extinct volcano. Mount Guallatiri, in Chile, is the world's highest active volcano – it last erupted in 1969.

The higher you climb, the cooler it is. And the further you travel from the Equator, the cooler it is. Therefore, the snowline in southern Chile is *much* lower than in northern Chile.

Sheep farming in Patagonia, Argentina. *Southern Argentina has a cool, dry climate. Very few people live there – but lots of sheep roam the extensive grasslands. There are almost as many sheep in Argentina as there are people.*

Argentina means 'silvery' in Spanish: some of the early settlers came to mine silver. But today, Argentina's most important product is cattle. Cool grasslands called the Pampas are ideal for cattle-grazing.

Argentina is a varied country: the northwest is hot and dry, and the south is cold and dry (see photograph). The frontier with Chile runs high along the top of the Andes.

Buenos Aires, the capital city, is the biggest city in South America; it has 10 million people. The name means 'good air', but petrol fumes have now polluted the air.

Paraguay and **Uruguay** are two countries with small populations. Each country has under five million people. Nearly half the population of Uruguay lives in the capital city, Montevideo, which is on the coast. In contrast Paraguay is completely landlocked. Animal-farming is the most important occupation in both these countries.

THE PACIFIC

This map shows half the world. Guess which place is furthest from a continent: it is somewhere in the south Pacific. The Pacific also includes the deepest place in the world: the Mariana Trench (11,022 metres deep). It would take over an hour for a steel ball weighing half a kilogram to fall to the bottom!

There are thousands of islands in the Pacific Ocean. Some are volcanic mountains, while many others are low, flat coral islands. Coral also grows round the volcanoes (see photograph below).

A few islands have valuable minerals – for example Nauru (phosphates) and Bougainville (copper). But most islanders are occupied in farming. Many tropical crops grow well; sugarcane, bananas and pineapple are important exports. Islands big enough for a full-sized airport, such as Fiji, the Samoan islands, Tahiti, and Hawaii (see page 66), now get many globe-trotting tourists.

Moorea from the air. *The coral reef can be clearly seen around this island in French Polynesia; the reef makes it difficult for ships to reach the land.*

The island is steep and rugged: it is an old volcano. Notice the deep valleys dug by rivers. The white patches are clouds, not snow.

▽

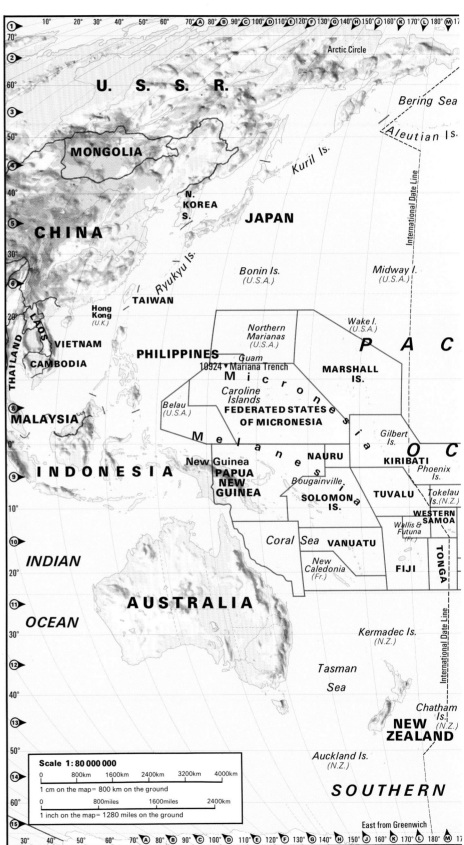

Easter Island, South Pacific. *These huge stone sculptures each weigh about 50 tonnes! They were cut long ago with simple stone axes, and lifted with ropes and ramps – an amazing achievement for people who had no metal, no wheels and no machines.*

Look for Easter Island on the map (in square U 11): it is one of the remotest places in the world. It is now owned by Chile, 3860 kilometres away in South America.

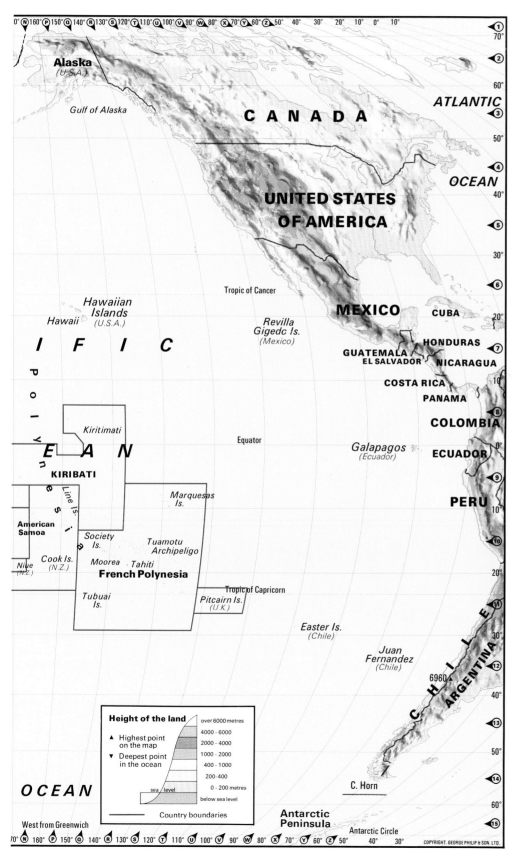

0° Ⓝ 160° Ⓟ 150° Ⓠ 140° Ⓡ 130° Ⓢ 120° Ⓣ 110° Ⓤ 100° Ⓥ 90° Ⓦ 80° Ⓧ 70° Ⓨ 60° Ⓩ 50° 40° 30° 20° 10° 0° 10°

Alaska (U.S.A.)

Gulf of Alaska

C A N A D A

ATLANTIC

UNITED STATES OF AMERICA

OCEAN

Tropic of Cancer

Hawaiian Islands
Hawaii (U.S.A.)

Revilla Gigedc Is. (Mexico)

MEXICO

CUBA

P A C I F I C

HONDURAS
GUATEMALA
EL SALVADOR
NICARAGUA
COSTA RICA
PANAMA

COLOMBIA

Kiritimati

Equator

Galapagos (Ecuador)

ECUADOR

O C E A N

KIRIBATI

Line Is.

Marquesas Is.

PERU

P o l y n e s i a

American Samoa

Society Is.

Tuamotu Archipeligo

Niue (N.Z.)
Cook Is. (N.Z.)

Moorea Tahiti

French Polynesia

Tropic of Capricorn

Tubuai Is.

Pitcairn Is. (U.K.)

Easter Is. (Chile)

Juan Fernandez (Chile)

6960

C H I L E
ARGENTINA

Height of the land
over 6000 metres
4000 - 6000
▲ Highest point on the map
2000 - 4000
▼ Deepest point in the ocean
1000 - 2000
400 - 1000
200 - 400
0 - 200 metres
sea level
below sea level
—— Country boundaries

O C E A N

C. Horn

West from Greenwich

Antarctic Peninsula
Antarctic Circle

70° Ⓝ 160° Ⓞ 150° Ⓠ 140° Ⓡ 130° Ⓢ 120° Ⓣ 110° Ⓤ 100° Ⓥ 90° Ⓦ 80° Ⓧ 70° Ⓨ 60° Ⓩ 50° 40° 30°

COPYRIGHT. GEORGE PHILIP & SON. LTD.

Most Pacific countries are large groups of small islands. Their boundaries are out at sea – just lines on a map. Kiribati is 33 small coral atolls spread over 5 million square kilometres of ocean. And the Solomon Islands stretch for 1450 kilometres. Imagine organizing something for the whole country!

Pacific stamps

The stamp from **French Polynesia** shows coconut-palms – and an outrigger canoe: you can see how this makes the dug-out canoe more stable at sea. In the background, there are canoes with sails.

In the highlands of **Papua New Guinea** (north of Australia), people live in round huts with thatched roofs. The stamp also shows the island's high, rugged mountains.

AUSTRALIA

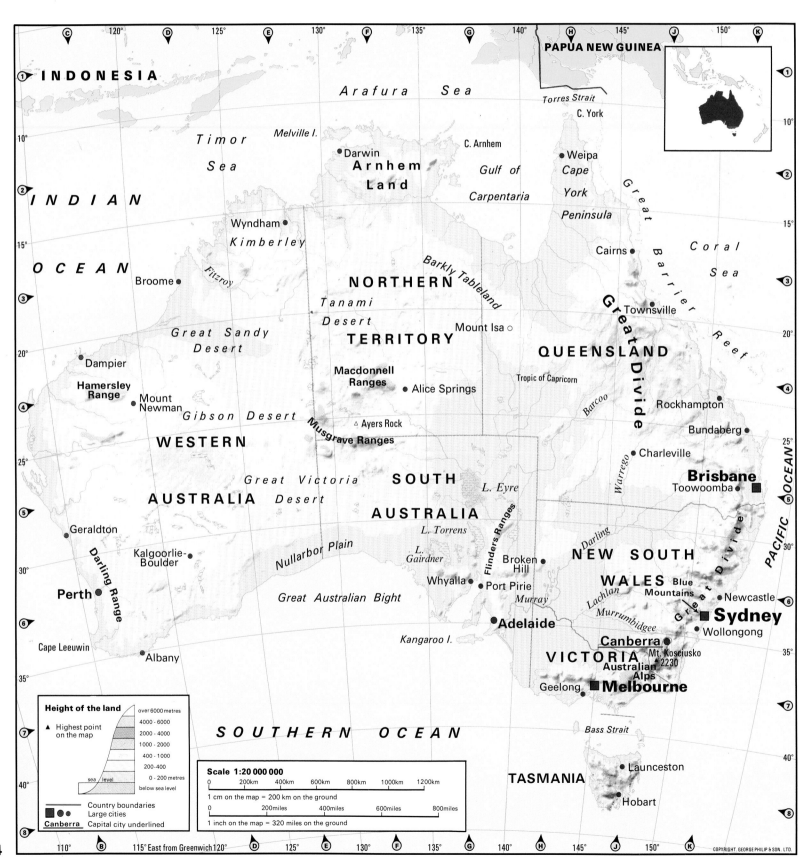

INDONESIA

Arafura Sea

PAPUA NEW GUINEA

Torres Strait

C. York

Timor

Melville I.

C. Arnhem

•Weipa

•Darwin

Arnhem Land

Gulf of

Cape

York

Peninsula

I N D I A N

Sea

O C E A N

Wyndham

Kimberley

Cairns

Coral

Sea

•Broome

Fitzroy

Barkly Tableland

NORTHERN

•Townsville

Great

Tanami

Desert

Mount Isa ○

Barrier

QUEENSLAND

Reef

•Dampier

Great Sandy Desert

TERRITORY

Great

Divide

Hamersley Range

Mount Newman

Macdonnell Ranges

•Alice Springs

Tropic of Capricorn

Barcoo

•Rockhampton

Gibson Desert

△ Ayers Rock

Bundaberg •

WESTERN

Musgrave Ranges

Warrego

•Charleville

Great Victoria

SOUTH

L. Eyre ○

Brisbane

AUSTRALIA

Desert

AUSTRALIA

Toowoomba •■

Geraldton •

L. Torrens

Darling

NEW SOUTH

Flinders Ranges

Kalgoorlie-Boulder •

Nullarbor Plain

L. Gairdner ○

Broken Hill

Lachlan

WALES

Blue Mountains

• Newcastle

Perth ■

Darling Range

Whyalla •

•Port Pirie

Murray

Murrumbidgee

Sydney ■

Great Australian Bight

•Adelaide ■

Wollongong •

Cape Leeuwin

Kangaroo I.

Canberra

VICTORIA Mt. Kosciusko

•Albany

Australian Alps ▲ 2230

Geelong •

Melbourne ■

S O U T H E R N   O C E A N

Bass Strait

TASMANIA

•Launceston

•Hobart

PACIFIC OCEAN

Height of the land

▲ Highest point on the map

over 6000 metres
4000 - 6000
2000 - 4000
1000 - 2000
400 - 1000
200 - 400
0 - 200 metres
below sea level

sea level

■ ● ● ── Country boundaries
Large cities
Canberra Capital city underlined

Scale 1:20 000 000

0   200km   400km   600km   800km   1000km   1200km

1 cm on the map = 200 km on the ground

0   200miles   400miles   600miles   800miles

1 inch on the map = 320 miles on the ground

110°   115° East from Greenwich 120°   125°   130°   135°   140°   145°   150°

The Indian-Pacific Express

Town	Time	Day no.	Distance (kilometres)
Perth	21.00	1	0
Kalgoorlie	07.00	2	657
Port Pirie	14.00	3	2439
Broken Hill	20.54	3	2836
Sydney	15.55	4	3961

It takes three nights and three days to cross Australia by train, from Perth to Sydney. The map shows you why the train is called the Indian-Pacific.

Australia is the world's largest island, but the smallest continent. It is the sixth-largest country in the world, smaller than the USA or Canada, but more than twice the size of India. Yet Australia has only about 16 million people. Most Australians are descended from people who came from Europe in the past 150 years.

The map shows that all the state capitals are on the coast, but Canberra, the national capital, is inland. Most Australians live in towns near the coast.

Only a few people live in the mountains or in the outback – the enormous area of semi-desert and desert that makes up most of the country. The few outback people live on huge sheep and cattle farms, in mining-towns, or on special reserves for the original Australians, the Aborigines. Yet the wool, the meat, and the minerals of the outback are important exports.

The Great Barrier Reef *is the world's largest living thing! It is an area of coral over 2000 kilometres long, which grows in the warm sea near the coast of Queensland.*

Ayers Rock *is in the heart of the desert in central Australia. Nothing grows on its steep sides. At sunset, it looks bright red!*

Christmas 'down under' *is in midsummer. Justine's stamp shows a typical Australian Christmas at the seaside, with swimming and sunbathing. But she didn't forget Father Christmas, with his red coat and his reindeer!*

Animals in Australia. *Australia is not joined to any other continent. It has been a separate island for millions of years, and has developed its own unique wildlife.*

The first stamps for the whole of Australia showed the country's most famous animal (far right). The kangaroo is a marsupial, which means 'pouched' – mother has her

own 'pocket' for baby Roo! Most of the world's marsupials live in Australia. Four of these animals are endangered species: they will die out unless they are protected.

NEW ZEALAND

The Antipodes

New Zealand is on the opposite side of the Earth from Europe. This double map shows that the far north of New Zealand is at the same latitude as North Africa, and that the far south of New Zealand is at the same latitude as Paris.

The New Zealand flag includes the British flag, because it was a British colony for over 100 years. Most New Zealand families originally came from Britain. The stars are known as the Southern Cross.

The two main islands that make up New Zealand are 2000 kilometres east of Australia. Only 3½ million people live in the whole country. The capital is Wellington, near the centre of New Zealand, but the largest city is Auckland in the north.

The original inhabitants were the Maoris, but now they are only about 8 per cent of the population. Some place-names are Maori words, such as Rotorua and Wanganui.

South Island is the largest island, but has fewer people than North Island. There are far more sheep than people! Mount Cook, the highest point in New Zealand (3764 metres), is in the spectacular Southern Alps. Tourists visit the far south to see the glaciers and fjords. The fast-flowing rivers are used for hydro-electricity.

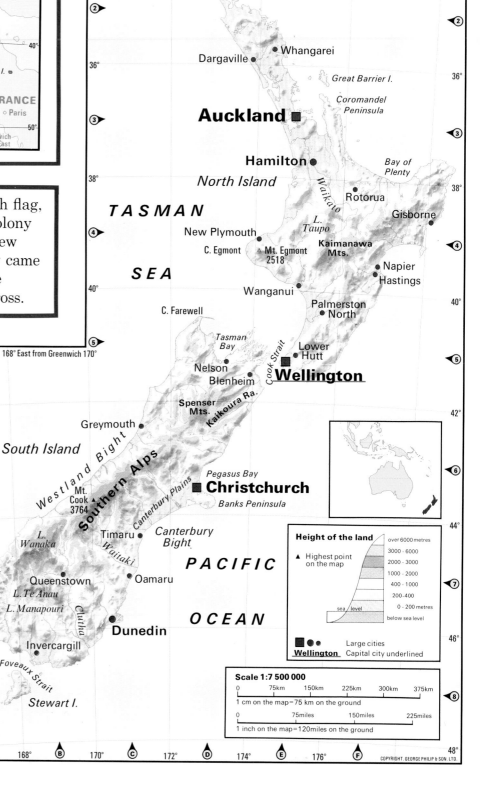

COPYRIGHT. GEORGE PHILIP & SON. LTD.

A geothermal power-station *in North Island. In this volcanic area there is natural hot steam underground which can be piped to power-stations to produce electricity.*

New Zealand exports

These stamps show some major exports: pine trees become sawn timber for export (10c); sheep's wool is spun for export (18c); the 20 cent stamp shows cattle hides and skins being lifted onto a ship; while the 25 cent stamp shows cartons of New Zealand butter being loaded. Notice the snow-covered volcanic mountain in the background.

North Island has a warmer climate than South Island. In some places you can see hot springs and boiling mud pools and there are also volcanoes. Fine trees and giant ferns grow in the forests, but much of the forest has been cleared for farming. Cattle are kept on the rich grasslands for meat and milk. Many different kinds of fruit grow well, including apples and kiwi-fruit.

Sheep grazing on the Canterbury Plains, *in South Island. New Zealand lamb is exported to Europe and North America in refrigerated ships. In the distance are the snow-covered Southern Alps. This great mountain range has glaciers, fjords and ski-slopes.*

ANTARCTIC

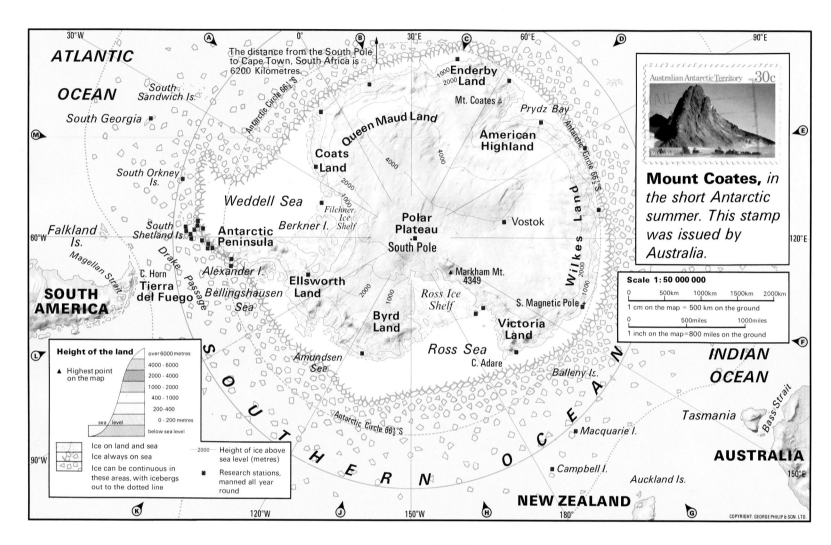

The distance from the South Pole to Cape Town, South Africa is 6200 Kilometres.

ATLANTIC OCEAN

South Sandwich Is.

South Georgia

South Orkney Is.

Weddell Sea

Falkland Is.

Magellan Strait

South Shetland Is.

C. Horn
Tierra del Fuego

SOUTH AMERICA

Drake Passage

Alexander I.

Bellingshausen Sea

Antarctic Peninsula

Berkner I.

Filchner Ice Shelf

Coats Land

Queen Maud Land

Enderby Land

Mt. Coates

Prydz Bay

American Highland

Polar Plateau

South Pole

Vostok

Markham Mt. 4349

Ellsworth Land

Byrd Land

Ross Ice Shelf

S. Magnetic Pole

Victoria Land

Amundsen Sea

Ross Sea

C. Adare

Balleny Is.

Wilkes Land

INDIAN OCEAN

Tasmania

Bass Strait

Macquarie I.

AUSTRALIA

Campbell I.

Auckland Is.

NEW ZEALAND

SOUTHERN OCEAN

Antarctic Circle 66½°S

Antarctic Circle 66½°S

Mount Coates, *in the short Antarctic summer. This stamp was issued by Australia.*

Australian Antarctic Territory 30c

Scale 1:50 000 000

| 0 | 500km | 1000km | 1500km | 2000km |

1 cm on the map = 500 km on the ground

| 0 | 500miles | 1000miles |

1 inch on the map = 800 miles on the ground

Height of the land

over 6000 metres
▲ Highest point on the map
4000 - 6000
2000 - 4000
1000 - 2000
400 - 1000
200 - 400
0 - 200 metres
sea level
below sea level

Ice on land and sea
Ice always on sea
Ice can be continuous in these areas, with icebergs out to the dotted line

2000 — Height of ice above sea level (metres)

■ Research stations, manned all year round

COPYRIGHT. GEORGE PHILIP & SON. LTD.

Emperor penguins *with chicks. Penguins cannot fly, but they can swim very well. The parents use their feet to protect the eggs and chicks from the cold ice! No land animals live in Antarctica, but the ocean is full of fish, which provide food for penguins, seals and whales.*

▽

Fact box: Antarctica

5th largest continent – about 13,900,000 square kilometres

Surrounded by cold **seas**
South Pole **first reached** in 1911

Antarctica is the continent surrounding the South Pole. It is the coldest, windiest and iciest place in the world! It is also very isolated, as the map shows.

No people live in Antarctica permanently. Some scientists work in research stations.

Everything that is needed in Antarctica has to be brought in during the short summer. From November to January, icebreakers can reach the land. But huge icebergs are always a danger. In winter (May to July) it is always dark, the sea is frozen, and people have to face extreme cold and dangerous blizzards.

ARCTIC

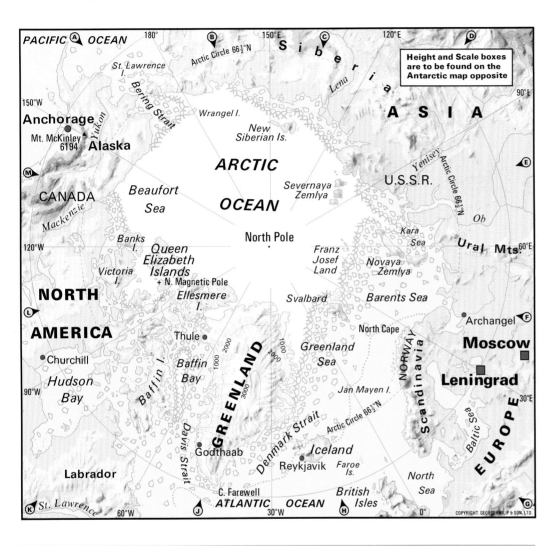

The Arctic is an ocean, which is frozen throughout the winter. It is surrounded by the northernmost areas of three continents, but Greenland is the only truly Arctic country.

For most of the year the land is snow-covered. During the short summer, when the sun never sets, the snow and the frozen topsoil melt. But the deeper soil is still frozen, so the land is very marshy. This treeless landscape is called the tundra.

The reindeer and caribou can be herded or hunted, but farming is impossible. In recent years, rich mineral deposits have been found. Canada, the USA and USSR have military bases facing each other across the Arctic Ocean.

▲
Eskimos. *The Inuit (Eskimos) have lived in the Arctic for thousands of years by hunting and fishing. These men* (left) *are resting their husky dogs which are trained to pull sledges.*

The Inuit only build igloos as emergency shelters. Most of them live in wooden buildings that are well insulated against the cold, like the Greenland family (above), *and most are more likely to travel by motorized skidoo than by sledge. Many work in mining camps, military bases and weather stations.*

Fact box: Arctic

4th largest ocean – about 14,000,000 square kilometres

World record for least sunshine and tallest iceberg
Surrounded by cold **land**
North Pole **first reached** in 1909

89

QUIZ

Name the island

The name of the continent where each island is found is marked on each outline. Do you know (*a*) the name of each island and (*b*) to which country each island belongs (or are they island countries)?

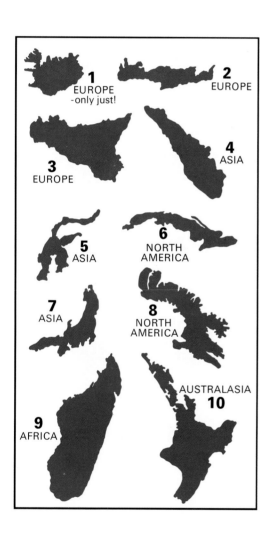

1 EUROPE -only just!
2 EUROPE
3 EUROPE
4 ASIA
5 ASIA
6 NORTH AMERICA
7 ASIA
8 NORTH AMERICA
9 AFRICA
10 AUSTRALASIA

Name the country

There is a long, thin country in almost every continent. Can you name the countries shown here – and name the continent in which they are found? (If you need help, look at pages 8–9 for a map of the countries of the world.)

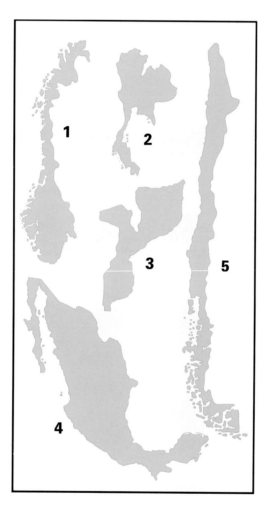

1
2
3
4
5

A mystery message

Use the map of the countries of the world on pages 8–9 to decode this message. Each missing word is all or part of the name of a country. (For some answers, letters have to be taken out of or added to the name of the country.)

I was _____a__ (east of Austria), so I bought a large _____ (east of Greece), some _____ns (east of Norway) and a bottle of ____ugal (west of Spain). Finally, I ate an ___land (west of Norway) -cream. I enjoyed my _e__i (east of Mauritania), but afterwards I began to _____earia (south of Romania) and I got a bad s_____ (south of France). A o____ (east of Saudi Arabia) told me: 'Just eat Philip_____sapples (south of Taiwan) and __gypt (east of Libya), cooked in a Ja____ (east of Korea). Tomorrow you can eat a Ghban___ (east of Ivory Coast) and some _____ (east of Peru) nuts. It shouldn't ____a Rica (west of Panama) you too much.' I said: 'You must be ___agascar (east of Mozambique)! I think I've got ____ysr__ (north of Indonesia). I'll have __/__ (west of Benin) to a doctor quickly, otherwise I'll soon be _____sea (lake between Israel and Jordan).' Happily, the doctor __bared (island country south of USA) me, so I am still M__d___s (islands west of Sri Lanka) today!

Oceans and seas

What ocean would you cross on an aeroplane journey. . .
1 From Australia to the USA?
2 From Brazil to South Africa?
3 From Canada to the USSR?
4 From Madagascar to Indonesia?

90   5 From Mexico to Portugal?

What sea would you cross on an aeroplane journey. . .
6 From Saudi Arabia to Egypt?
7 From Korea to Japan?
8 From Denmark to the United Kingdom?
9 From Vietnam to the Philippines?
10 From Cuba to Colombia?

Places in Asia

Move the letters to find:

Countries
RAIN; CHAIN; MOAN; AWAIT N.
Capital cities
ANIMAL; I HELD; A BULK
KEG NIP; LOUSE; DIARY H.

Find the colour

Each answer is a colour. Use the atlas index and the maps to help you.

Cover the right-hand column with a piece of paper and try to answer the left-hand column only. Award yourself *2* points for each correct answer to the left-hand column only, or *1* point if you used the clues in both columns.

1 A sea between Egypt and Saudi Arabia. . .

2 A huge island east of Canada. . .

3 The sea between Turkey and the USSR. . .

4 The sea between Korea and China. . .

5 The sea on which Archangel lies, in the USSR. . .

6 A town in southern France which is also a fruit. . .

7 The tributary of the River Nile that flows from Ethiopia to Khartoum (Sudan). . .

. . .and the river on the border of Oklahoma and Texas, USA.

. . .and a bay on the west side of Lake Michigan, USA.

. . .and a forest in Germany.

. . .and a (stony?) river in Wyoming, USA.

. . .and the river flowing north from Lake Victoria to Khartoum (Sudan).

. . .and the river which makes the border between South Africa and Namibia.

. . .and a mountain ridge in eastern USA.

How well do you know the states of the USA?

All the answers can be found on the maps on pages 62–3 and 66–9. Do not include Alaska and Hawaii.

1 Which is the *biggest* state?
2 Which is the *smallest* state?
3 Which state reaches furthest *north*? (careful!)
4 Which state reaches furthest *south*?
5 Which state reaches furthest *west*?
6 Which state reaches furthest *east*?
7 Which state is split into two by a lake?
8 Which state is split into two by an inlet of the sea?
9 Which two states are perfect rectangles in shape?
10 Which state is shaped like a saucepan?
11 In which state would you be if you visited Lake Huron?
12 In which state would you be if you visited Lake Ontario?
13 In which state would you be if you visited the Great Salt Lake?
14 In which state would you be if you visited the Mississippi delta?

15 Which state in *northern* USA is called South   ?
16 Which state in *southern* USA is called North   ?
17 There is only one place in the USA where four states meet: which states?
18 How many states have a border with Mexico?
19 How many states have a coastline on the Pacific?
20 How many states have a coastline on the Gulf of Mexico?

Great rivers of Europe

Use pages 18–39 to discover which great river flows through or near each pair of towns or cities.
1 Vienna, Austria and Budapest, Hungary.
2 Rotterdam, Netherlands and Bonn, Germany.
3 Avignon, France and Lyons, France.
4 Worcester, England and Gloucester, England.
5 Toledo, Spain and Lisbon, Portugal.

Things To Do

Where do the things you use come from?

What do you and your family use, eat or wear from different countries of the world? In this atlas you will find lists of some items we have found (pages 27 and 37). Now you can do some spotting.

Collect stamps with a theme

A stamp collection soon grows. Try a *thematic* collection: choose a theme (topic) and collect stamps on that theme. For example, you could collect:
Flags on stamps. Togo had a flag stamp for Independence Day.

Map stamps: small islands often issue map stamps to show everyone where they are!

Traditional crafts on stamps: this Zambian thatcher is using a home-made ladder.

Make your own coin collection

Ask people who have been abroad for any foreign coins they do not want – you will have an instant collection! If you cannot have the coins to keep, you could make pencil or crayon rubbings on thin paper. Look at the pictures of coins in the atlas. Look at your coins for examples of languages; crops; famous buildings; historic events. . . .

INDEX

How to Use this Index

The first number given after each name or topic is the page number; then a letter and another number tell you which square of the map you should look at.

For example, Abidjan is in square B2 on page 56. Find B at the top or bottom of the map on page 56 and put a finger on it. Put another finger on the number 2 at the side of the map. Move your fingers in from the edge of

the map and they will meet in square B2. Abidjan will now be easy to find. It is the capital city of the Ivory Coast, a country in West Africa.

If a name goes through more than one square, the square given in the index is the one in which the biggest part of the name falls.
Names like *Gulf of Mexico* and *Cape Horn* are in the Index index as *Mexico, Gulf of* and *Horn, Cape.*

Aachen 28 B3
Aalborg 22 C4
Aarhus 22 B4
Aberdeen 20 F2
Aberystwyth 20 D4
Abidjan 56 B2
Abu Dhabi 42 E3
Abuja 56 C2
Acapulco 73 C3
Accra 56 B2
Achill Sound 20 A3
Aconcagua 81 C3
Adamawa Highlands
  56 D2
Adana 42 C2
Adare, Cape 88 G
Addis Ababa 59 C2
Adelaide 84 H7
Aden 42 D4
Aden, Gulf of 59 D1
Adriatic Sea 33 E3
Aegean Sea 35 C3
Afghanistan 44 B1
Africa 52
Agades 55 D3
Agra 44 C2
Ahmadabad 44 C2
Ahvaz 42 D2
Air 55 D3
Aix 26 G5
Ajaccio 33 B4
Akita 51 D3
Alabama 69 C3
Aland Islands 22 D3
Alaska 66 D2
Alaska Range 66 C2
Al Aziziyah 55 E1
Albacete 30 E4
Albania 35 B2
Albany (Australia) 84 C7
Albany (U.S.A.) 69 D2
Alberta 65 G4
Alborg 61 A2
Alboran 30 D6
Albuquerque 71 C3
Alderney 26 C2
Aleppo 42 C2
Alesund 22 B3
Aleutian Islands 82 L3
Alexander Island 88 L
Alexandria 55 F1
Algarve 30 A5
Algeria 55 D2

Algiers 55 D1
Alicante 30 E4
Alice Springs 84 G4
Al Jawf 55 F2
Alkmaar 24 C2
Alma Ata 38 M4
Almeria 30 D5
Alps 33 C1
Alsace 26 H2
Altai Mountains 48 C2
Amarillo 71 C3
Amazon River 79 E3
American Highland 88 D
American Samoa 83 N10
Amiens 26 E2
Amman 42 M2
Amritsar 44 C1
Amsterdam 24 D2
Amundsen Sea 88 K
Amur, River 38 R3
Anadyr Range 38 W2
Anatolia 18 P7
Anchorage 66 D2
Ancona 33 D3
Andalusia 30 C5
Andaman Islands 46 A2
Andes 76 C3
Andorra 30 F2
Angara, River 38 N3
Angers 26 D3
Anglesey 20 D4
Angola 61 A2
Angoulême 26 E4
Anguilla 74 F3
Ankara 42 C2
Annapurna 44 D2
Annobon 56 C3
Anshan 48 F2
Antananarivo 61 D2
Antarctic 12-13, 88
Antarctic Peninsula 88 M
Anticosti Island 65 M5
Antigua & Barbuda 74 F3
Antisiranana 61 D2
Antofagasta 81 B2
Antwerp 24 C3
Aomori 51 D2
Apennines 33 D3
Appalachian Mountains
  69 C3
Arabia 40 H6
Arabian Sea 40 K7
Arafura Sea 84 F1

Aral Sea 38 J4
Archangel 38 H2
Arctic 12-13, 89
Arctic Ocean 89
Ardennes 24 D5
Arequipa 79 C4
Argentina 81 C3
Arizona 71 B3
Arkansas 69 B3
Arkansas River 69 B3
Armagh 20 C3
Armenia 19 R6
Arnhem 24 D2
Arnhem, Cape 84 G2
Arnhem Land 84 F2
Arran 20 D3
Aruba 74 D4
Asahigawa 51 D2
Ascension 9 M4
Asia 40
Asmera 59 C1
Assal, Lake 52 G4
Asuncion 81 D2
Aswan 55 G2
Asyut 55 F2
Atacama Desert 81 B2
Athabasca Lake 65 H3
Athens 35 C3
Athlone 20 C4
Atlanta 69 C3
Atlas Mountains 55 C1
Atmosphere 4-5
Auckland 86 D3
Auckland Islands 88 G
Augsburg 28 D4
Austin 69 B3
Australia 84
Australian Alps 84 J7
Austria 28 E5
Auvergne 26 F4
Avignon 26 G5
Avon, River 20 F4
Axel Heiberg Island 65 K2
Ayers Rock 84 F5
Azerbaijan 19 S6
Azores 55 A1

Badajoz 30 B4
Baffin Bay 65 M2
Baffin Island 65 L2
Baghdad 42 D2
Bahamas 74 C2

Bahia Blanca 81 C3
Bahrain 42 E3
Baku 38 H5
Balaton, Lake 36 F5
Balearic Islands 30 F4
Bali 46 C4
Balikpapan 46 C4
Balkan Mountains 35 C2
Balkhash, Lake 38 L4
Balleny Islands 88 G
Baltic Sea 22 D4
Baltimore 69 D3
Bamako 55 C3
Banda Sea 46 D4
Bandung 46 B4
Bangalore 44 C3
Bangka 46 B4
Bangkok 46 B2
Bangladesh 44 E2
Bangui 59 A2
Banjarmasin 46 C4
Banjul 56 A1
Banks Island 65 F2
Banks Peninsula 86 D6
Barbados 74 G4
Barcelona 30 G3
Barcoo, River 84 H4
Barents Sea 38 G1
Bari 33 F4
Barkly Tableland 84 G3
Barquisimeto 79 D2
Barranquilla 79 C1
Barrow, Cape 66 C1
Basle 33 A1
Basque Provinces 30 D2
Basra 42 D2
Bass Strait 84 J7
Bastia 33 B3
Bathurst, Cape 65 F2
Baton Rouge 69 B3
Bavaria 28 D4
Baykal, Lake 38 Q3
Bayonne 26 D5
Beaufort Sea 65 D2
Beersheba 42 L3
Beira 61 C2
Beirut 42 C2
Belau 82 G8
Belcher Islands 65 K4
Belem 79 F3
Belfast 20 D3
Belgium 24 C4
Belgrade 35 B2

Belize 73 D3
Bellingshausen Sea 88 L
Belmopan 73 D3
Belo Horizonte 79 F4
Bengal, Bay of 40 M7
Benghazi 55 E1
Benin 56 C2
Benin, Bight of 56 C2
Ben Nevis 20 D2
Benue, River 56 C2
Bergen 22 B3
Bering Sea 82 L3
Bering Strait 89 A
Berkner Island 88 M
Berlin 28 E2
Bermuda 62 N5
Bern 33 A1
Besanc-con 26 H3
Bethlehem 42 L3
Bhutan 44 E2
Bialystok 36 H2
Bida 56 C2
Bielefeld 28 C2
Bielsko-Biala 36 F4
Bie Plateau 61 A2
Big Timber 71 B2
Bilbao 30 D2
Billings 71 C2
Bioko 56 C2
Birmingham (U.K.) 20 F4
Birmingham (U.S.A.)
  69 C3
Biscay, Bay of 18 G5
Bissau 56 A1
Bitola 35 C2
Black Forest 28 C4
Black Hills 71 C2
Black Sea 18 P6
Blanc, Mont 26 H4
Blantyre 61 C2
Blenheim 86 D5
Bloemfontein 61 B3
Blue Mountains 84 K6
Blue Nile 55 G3
Blue Ridge 69 C3
Bodo 22 C2
Bogota 79 C2
Bohemia 36 D4
Bohemian Forest 36 C4
Boise 71 B2
Bolivia 79 D4
Bologna 33 C3
Bolzano 33 C1

Bombay 44 C3
Bonifacio, Strait of 33 B4
Bonin Islands 82 H6
Bonn 28 B3
Bonny, Bight of 56 C2
Boothia, Gulf of 65 K3
Bordeaux 26 D4
Borneo 46 C3
Bornholm 22 D5
Bosporus 35 D2
Boston 69 D2
Bothnia, Gulf of 22 E3
Botswana 61 B3
Bouake 56 B2
Bougainville 82 J9
Boulogne 26 E1
Bournemouth 20 E5
Bradford 20 E4
Brahmaputra, River
  48 N3
Brasilia 79 F4
Brasov 35 D1
Bratislava 36 E4
Brazil 79 E4
Brazilian Highlands 79 F4
Brazzaville 59 A3
Bremen 28 C2
Brescia 33 C2
Brest 26 B2
Bridgetown 74 G4
Brighton 20 G5
Brindisi 33 G4
Brisbane 84 K5
Bristol 20 E5
Bristol Channel 20 E5
British Columbia 65 F4
British Isles 18 E4
Brittany 26 C2
Brno 36 E4
Broken Hill 84 G6
Brooks Range 66 C2
Broome 84 D3
Bruges 24 B3
Brunei 46 C3
Brunswick 28 D2
Brussels 24 C4
Bucaramanga 79 C2
Bucharest 35 C2
Budapest 36 F5
Buenos Aires 81 C3
Buffalo 69 D2

Bug, River 36 G2
Bujumbura 59 C3
Bukavu 59 B3
Bulawayo 61 C3
Bulgaria 35 D2
Bundaberg 84 K4
Burgas 35 D2
Burgos 30 D2
Burgundy 26 G3
Burkina Faso 56 B1
Burma 46 A1
Burundi 59 C3
Bydgoszcz 36 E2
Byelorussia 19 N4
Byrd Land 88 J
Bytom 36 F3

Cabinda 59 A3
Cabora Bassa Dam
  61 C2
Caceres 30 C4
Cadiz 30 B5
Caen 26 D2
Cagliari 33 B5
Caicos Islands 74 D2
Cairns 84 J3
Cairo 55 F1
Calais 26 F1
Calcutta 44 D2
Calgary 65 G4
Cali 79 C2
California 71 A3
California, Gulf of 73 A2
Callao 79 C4
Camaguey 74 C2
Cambodia 46 B2
Cambrian Mountains
  20 E4
Cambridge 20 G4
Cameroon 56 D2
Cameroon, Mount 56 C2
Campbell Island 88 G
Campeche, Gulf of 73 C3
Canada 65 J4
Canal 55, 72
Canary Islands 55 B2
Canaveral, Cape 69 D4
Canberra 84 J7
Cannes 26 H5
Cantabrian Mountains
  30 C2
Canterbury 20 G5

Canterbury Bight 86 D7
Canterbury Plains 86 D6
Canton 48 E4
Canyon 70
Cape Breton Island 65 N5
Cape Town 61 A4
Cape York Peninsula 84 H2
Caracas 79 D1
Carcassonne 26 F5
Cardiff 20 E5
Caribbean Sea 74 C4
Carletonville 61 B3
Carlisle 20 E3
Caroline Islands 82 H8
Carpathian Mountains 36 G4
Carpentaria, Gulf of 84 G2
Cars 29, 32
Cartagena 30 E5
Carthage 55 D1
Casablanca 55 B1
Cascade Range 71 A2
Casper 71 C2
Caspian Sea 40 J4
Castellon 30 F4
Catalonia 30 F3
Catania 33 E6
Caucasus 38 H4
Cayenne 79 E2
Cebu 46 D2
Celebes 46 D4
Celebes Sea 46 D3
Central African Republic 59 B2
Central America 62 K7
Ceram 46 D4
Ceuta 30 C6
Cevennes 26 F4
Chad 55 E3
Chad, Lake 55 E3
Champagne 26 G2
Changchun 48 F2
Changsha 48 E4
Channel Islands 26 C2
Chari, River 55 E3
Charleroi 24 C4
Charleston 69 C3
Charleville 84 J5
Charlotte 69 D3
Chartres 26 E2
Chatham Islands 82 M13
Chattanooga 69 C3
Chelyabinsk 38 K3
Chemnitz 28 E3
Chengchow 48 E3
Chengtu 48 D3
Cherbourg 26 D2
Chiang Mai 46 A2
Chicago 69 B2
Chichen Itza 73 D2
Chidley, Cape 65 M4
Chile 81 B3
China 48 C3
Chita 38 Q3
Chittagong 44 E2
Christchurch 86 D6
Christmas Island 9 V4
Chungking 48 D4
Churchill 65 J4
Cincinnati 69 C3
Citlaltepetl 73 C3
Ciudad Juarez 73 B1
Clermont Ferrand 26 F4
Cleveland 69 D2
Cluj 35 C1
Clutha, River 86 B7
Coast Range 71 A3
Coats Land 88 A
Cocos Islands 9 U4
Cod, Cape 69 E2
Coffee 73
Coimbatore 44 C3
Coimbra 30 A3
Cologne 28 B3
Colombia 79 C2
Colombo 44 C4
Colorado 71 C3
Colorado River 71 B3

Columbia, River 71 A2
Columbus 69 C3
Communism Peak 38 K4
Comorin, Cape 44 C4
Comoros 61 D2
Conakry 56 A2
Concepcion 81 B3
Congo 59 A3
Connecticut 69 D2
Constance, Lake 28 C5
Constanta 35 D2
Constantine 55 D1
Continents 5, 8
Cook Islands 83 N11
Cook, Mount 86 B6
Cook Strait 86 E5
Copenhagen 22 C4
Coral Sea 84 J3
Cordoba (Argentina) 81 C3
Cordoba (Spain) 30 C5
Corfu 35 B3
Cork 20 B5
Coromandel Peninsula 86 F3
Corsica 33 B3
Cosenza 33 F5
Costa Blanca 30 E4
Costa Brava 30 G3
Costa del Sol 30 C5
Costa Rica 73 D3
Cotonou 56 C2
Cotswolds 20 F5
Countries 8, 9
Coventry 20 F4
Craiova 35 C2
Crete 35 D4
Creus, Cape 30 G2
Crozet Islands 9 R5
Crust (earth) 5
Cuando, River 61 B2
Cuba 74 C2
Cubango River 61 A2
Curacao 74 E4
Curitiba 81 F5
Cuzco 79 C4
Cyprus 42 J1
Czechoslovakia 36 E4
Czestochowa 36 F3

Dacca 44 E2
Dakar 56 A1
Dakhla 55 B2
Dalian 48 F3
Dallas 69 B3
Damascus 42 C2
Dampier 84 C4
Dams 60
Da Nang 46 B2
Danube River 35 D2
Dardanelles 35 D3
Dar es Salaam 59 D3
Dargaville 86 D2
Darjeeling 44 D2
Darling Range 84 C6
Darling, River 84 H6
Darwin 84 F2
Davao 46 D3
Davis Strait 65 N3
Dawson 65 E3
Dead Sea 42 M3
Death Valley 71 B3
Debrecen 36 G5
Deccan 44 C3
Delaware 69 D3
Delhi 44 C2
Demavend 42 E2
Den Helder 24 C2
Denmark 22 B4
Denver 71 C3
Derby 20 F4
Desert 13, 15, 53, 54-5, 80
Detroit 69 C2
Devon Island 65 K2
Diamonds 61
Dieppe 26 E2
Dijon 26 G3
Dinaric Alps 35 B2

District of Columbia 69 D3
Djerid, Lake 55 D1
Djibouti 59 D1
Dodecanese 35 D3
Dodoma 59 C3
Dominica 74 F3
Dominican Republic 74 D3
Dondra Head 44 C4
Donetsk 38 H4
Dordogne, River 26 E4
Dordrecht 24 C3
Dortmund 28 C3
Douai 26 F1
Douala 56 D2
Douglas 20 D3
Douro, River 30 B3
Dover 20 G5
Dover, Strait of 20 G5
Drakensberg Mountains 61 B3
Drava, River 35 B1
Dresden 28 F3
Duarte, Pico 74 D3
Dublin 20 E4
Dubrovnik 35 B2
Duero, River 30 D3
Duisburg 28 B3
Duluth 69 B2
Dundee 20 E2
Dunedin 86 C8
Dunkirk 26 F1
Durban 61 C4
Düsseldorf 28 B3
Dzungarian Desert 48 B2

Earth 4-5
Earthquakes 5
East China Sea 48 F4
Easter Islands 83 U11
Eastern Ghats 44 C3
East London 61 B4
Ebro, River 30 E3
Echo Bay 65 G3
Ecuador 79 C3
Edinburgh 20 E3
Edmonton 65 H4
Edward, Lake 59 B3
Egadi Islands 33 C6
Egmont, Cape 86 D4
Egmont, Mount 86 E4
Egypt 55 F2
Eilat 42 C3
Eindhoven 24 D3
El Aaiun 55 B2
Elba 33 C3
Elbe, River 28 C2
Elblag 36 F1
Elbrus, Mount 38 H4
Elburz Mountains 42 E2
Eleuthera Island 74 C1
El Fasher 55 F3
Ellesmere Land 65 L2
Ellsworth Land 88 L
El Obeid 55 F3
El Paso 71 C3
El Salvador 73 D3
Ems, River 28 B2
Enderby Land 88 C
England 20 F4
English Channel 26 D1
Enschede 24 E2
Equator 5, 13
Equatorial Guinea 56 C2
Erfurt 28 D3
Erie, Lake 69 C2
Eritrea 59 C1
Esbjerg 22 B4
Esfahan 42 E2
Essen 28 B3
Estonia 19 N3
Ethiopia 59 D2
Ethiopian Highlands 59 C2
Etna, Mount 33 E6
Etosha Pan 61 A2
Eugene 71 A2

Euphrates, River 42 D2
Europe 18
European Community 18-19, 96
Europoort 24 B3
Everest, Mount 48 B4
Everglades 69 C4
Evora 30 B4
Exeter 20 E5
Eyre, Lake 84 G5

Fairbanks 66 D2
Falkland Islands 81 C5
Farewell, Cape 86 D5
Fargo 69 B2
Faroe Islands 18 G2
Faults 5
Faya-Largeau 55 E3
F'Derik 55 B2
Fez 55 C1
Fiji 82 L10
Filchner Ice Shelf 88 M
Finisterre, Cape 30 A2
Finland 22 F3
Finland, Gulf of 22 F4
Firth of Forth 20 E2
Fish 31, 50, 52, 58
Fitzroy, River 84 D3
Flags 21, 37, 45, 66-7, 86
Flanders 24 B3
Flensburg 28 C1
Flinders Ranges 84 G6
Florence 33 C3
Flores Sea 46 C4
Florida 69 C4
Foggia 33 E4
Foochow 48 E4
Football 67, 70
Forests 15, 23, 39, 78
Fortaleza 79 F3
Fort McMurray 65 G4
Fort Worth 69 B3
Fouta Djalon 56 A1
Foveaux Strait 86 B8
Foxe Channel 65 K3
France 26 E3
Frankfurt 28 C3
Franz Josef Land 38 K1
Fraser River 65 F4
Freeport 74 C1
Freetown 56 A2
Freiburg 28 B5
French Guiana 79 E2
French Polynesia 83 R11
Fresno 71 A3
Frisian Islands 24 C1
Frontier 16, 19
Fuji, Mount 51 C3
Fukuoka 51 A4
Fukushima 51 D3
Fushun 48 F2

Gabon 56 D3
Gaborone 61 B3
Gairdner, Lake 84 F6
Galapagos Islands 79 B1
Galati 35 D1
Galilee, Sea of 42 M2
Galway 20 B4
Gambia 56 A1
Ganges, River 44 D2
Garda, Lake 33 C2
Garonne, River 26 D4
Gascony 26 D5
Gavle 22 D3
Gaza Strip 42 L3
Gdansk 36 F1
Geelong 84 H7
Geneva 33 A1
Geneva, Lake 33 A1
Genoa 33 B2
George Town 46 A3
Georgetown 79 E2
Georgia (U.S.A.) 69 C3

Georgia (U.S.S.R.) 19 R6
Gera 28 E3
Geraldton 84 C5
Germany 28 C4
Ghana 56 B2
Ghent 24 B3
Ghudamis 55 E2
Gibraltar 30 C5
Gibraltar, Strait of 30 B6
Gibson Desert 84 D4
Gifu 51 C3
Gijon 30 C2
Giza 55 F2
Glama, River 22 C3
Glasgow 20 D3
Gliwice 36 F3
Gloucester 20 E5
Gobi Desert 48 D2
Godavari, River 44 C3
Goiania 79 E4
Gold 61
Good Hope, Cape of 61 A4
Gorge 28, 70
Gorki 38 H3
Gothenburg 22 C4
Gotland 22 D4
Göttingen 28 C3
Gouda 24 C2
Gozo 33 E6
Gran Chaco 81 C2
Granada 30 D5
Gran Chaco 81 C2
Grand Bahama 74 C1
Grand Canyon 71 B3
Grand Cayman 74 B3
Graz 28 F5
Great Australia Bight 84 E6
Great Barrier Island 86 F3
Great Barrier Reef 84 J3
Great Basin 71 B3
Great Bear Lake 65 F3
Great Britain 18 G3
Great Divide 84 K6
Greater Antilles 74 C3
Great Khingan Mountains 48 E2
Great Lakes 62 L4
Great Plains 71 D2
Great Salt Lake 71 B2
Great Sandy Desert 84 D4
Great Slave Lake 65 G3
Great Victoria Desert 84 E5
Great Wall of China 48 D3
Greece 35 C3
Green Bay 69 C2
Greenland 89 J
Greenland Sea 89 G
Grenada 74 F4
Grenoble 26 H4
Greymouth 86 C6
Groningen 24 E1
Grossglockner 28 E5
Guadalajara 73 B2
Guadalquivir, River 30 C5
Guadarrama, Sierra de 30 D3
Guadeloupe 74 F3
Guadiana, River 30 B5
Guam 82 H7
Guardafui, Cape 59 E1
Guatemala 73 C3
Guatemala City 73 C3
Guayaquil 79 B3
Guernsey 26 C2
Guinea 56 A1
Guinea-Bissau 56 A1
Guinea, Gulf of 56 B2
Guyana 79 E2
Gyor 36 E5

Haarlem 24 C2
Hachinohe 51 D2
Haifa 42 L2
Hainan 48 E5

Haiphong 46 B1
Haiti 74 D3
Hakodate 51 D2
Halifax 65 M5
Halle 28 E3
Halmahera 46 D3
Hamamatsu 51 C4
Hamburg 28 C2
Hamersley Range 84 C4
Hamilton (Canada) 65 L5
Hamilton (N.Z.) 86 E3
Hanoi 46 B1
Hanover 28 C2
Harare 61 B2
Hardanger Fjord 22 B3
Harz Mountains 28 D3
Hastings 86 F4
Hatteras, Cape 62 M5
Havana 74 C2
Hawaii 66 F2
Hawaiian Islands 66 F1
Hebrides 20 C2
Heidelberg 28 C4
Helsinki 22 E3
Herat 44 B1
Himalayas 44 D2
Hindu Kush 44 C1
Hiroshima 51 B4
Hispaniola 74 D3
Hitachi 51 D3
Ho Chi Minh City 46 B2
Hobart 84 J8
Hoggar 55 D2
Hokkaido 51 D2
Holidays 31, 32, 34, 59, 75
Holyhead 20 D4
Honduras 73 D3
Hong Kong 48 E4
Honolulu 66 F1
Honshu 51 C3
Hook of Holland 24 B2
Horn, Cape 81 C5
Houston 69 B3
Huambo 61 A2
Huascaran 79 C3
Hudson Bay 65 K4
Hudson River 69 D2
Hudson Strait 65 L3
Huelva 30 B5
Hull 20 F4
Hungary 36 F5
Huron, Lake 69 C2
Hwang Ho, River 48 E3
Hyderabad (India) 44 C3
Hyderabad (Pakistan) 44 C2

Iasi 35 D1
Ibadan 56 C2
Iberian peninsula 18 G6
Ibiza 30 F4
Iceland 22 J2
Idaho 71 B2
Illinois 69 C2
Iloilo 46 D2
Inari, Lake 22 F2
India 44 C2
Indiana 69 C2
Indianapolis 69 C2
Indian Ocean 7
Indonesia 46 C4
Indore 44 C2
Indus, River 44 B2
Inland Sea 51 B4
Inn, River 28 E4
Innsbruck 28 D5
Interlaken 33 B1
International Date Line 82 L5
Invercargill 86 B8
Inverness 20 E2
Ionian Islands 35 B3
Ionian Sea 35 B3
Iowa 69 B2
Ipswich 20 G4
Iquitos 79 C3

Iraklion 35 C3
Iran 42 E2
Iraq 42 D2
Irbid 42 M2
Ireland 20 C4
Irish Sea 20 D4
Irkutsk 38 P3
Iron Gates 35 C2
Irrawaddy, River 46 A1
Irtysh, River 38 L3
Islamabad 44 C1
Islay 20 C3
Israel 42 M2
Istanbul 42 C1
Italy 33 D3
Ivory Coast 56 B2
Izmir 42 B2

Jabalpur 44 D2
Jacksonville 69 C3
Jaipur 44 C2
Jakarta 46 B4
Jamaica 74 C3
James Bay 65 K4
Japan 51 C3
Japan, Sea of 51 B3
Java 46 C4
Jedda 42 C3
Jerez 30 C5
Jersey 26 C2
Jerusalem 42 M3
Johannesburg 61 B3
Jonkoping 22 D4
Jordan 42 C2
Jordan, River 42 M2
Jotunheimen 22 B3
Juan Fernandez Island 83 W12
Juba 55 G4
Jucar, River 30 E4
Juneau 65 E4
Jura 26 G3
Jutland 22 B4

K2 44 C1
Kabul 44 B1
Kagoshima 51 A4
Kaikoura Range 86 D6
Kaimanawa Mountains 86 E4
Kalahari Desert 61 B3
Kalemie 59 B3
Kalgoorlie-Boulder 84 C6
Kamchatka Peninsula 38 U3
Kampala 59 C2
Kananga 59 B3
Kanazawa 51 C3
Kandahar 44 B1
Kangaroo Island 84 F7
Kano 56 C1
Kanpur 44 C2
Kansas 71 D3
Kansas City 69 B3
Kaohsiung 48 E4
Kapuas, River 46 C3
Karachi 44 B2
Karaganda 38 L4
Karakoram Range 44 C1
Kariba, Lake 61 B2
Karlsruhe 28 C4
Karoo 61 B4
Kasai, River 59 B3
Kashmir 44 C1
Kassel 28 C3
Katmandu 44 D2
Katowice 36 F3
Kattegat 22 C4
Kauai 66 E1
Kawasaki 51 C3
Kazan 38 H3
Keflavik 22 H2
Kemi 22 F2
Kemi, River 22 F2
Kentucky 69 C3
Kenya 59 C2
Kerguelen 9 S5

Kermadec Islands 82 L11
Key West 69 C4
Khabarovsk 38 S3
Kharkov 38 H3
Khartoum 55 G3
Kiel 28 C1
Kielce 36 G3
Kiev 38 G3
Kigali 59 C3
Kikwit 59 A3
Kilimanjaro 59 C3
Kimberley (Australia) 84 E3
Kimberley (S. Africa) 61 B3
Kinabalu 46 C3
Kingston 74 C3
Kinshasa 59 A3
Kiribati 82 L8
Kiritimati Island 83 P8
Kirkenes 22 F2
Kirov 38 J3
Kiruna 22 E2
Kisangani 59 B2
Kismayu 59 D3
Kiso, River 51 C3
Kisumu 59 C3
Kitakami, River 51 D3
Kitakyushu 51 A4
Kitwe 61 B2
Klagenfurt 28 F5
Kobe 51 B4
Koblenz 28 B3
Kola Peninsula 38 G2
Kolyma Range 38 U2
Korea Strait 51 A4
Kosciusko, Mount 84 J7
Kosice 36 G4
Krakatoa 46 B4
Krakow 36 G3
Krasnoyarsk 38 M3
Krishna, River 44 C3
Kristiansand 22 B4
Kuala Lumpur 46 B3
Kucing 46 C3
Kumamoto 51 B4
Kumasi 56 B2
Kunashir 51 E2
Kunlun Shan Mountains 48 B3
Kunming 48 D4
Kuopio 22 F3
Kuria Muria Islands 42 E4
Kuril Islands 82 J4
Kushiro 51 D2
Kuwait 42 D3
Kuybyshev 38 J3
Kweilin 48 E4
Kweiyang 48 D4
Kyoga, Lake 59 C2
Kyoto 51 C3
Kyushu 51 B4

Labe, River 36 D3
Labrador 65 M4
Laccadive Islands 44 C3
Lachlan, River 84 H6
La Coruna 30 A2
Ladoga, Lake 18 P3
Lagos (Nigeria) 56 C2
Lagos (Portugal) 30 A5
Lahore 44 C1
Lakes 63, 66, 77
Lanchow 48 D3
Land's End 20 C5
Languedoc 26 F5
Laos 46 B2
La Paz 79 D4
Lapland 22 E2
La Plata 81 D3
La Rochelle 26 D3
Las Palmas 55 B2
La Spezia 33 C2
Las Vegas 71 B3
Latvia 19 M3
Launceston 84 J8
Lausanne 33 A1
Lauterbrunnen 33 B1

Lebanon 42 C2
Leeds 20 F4
Leeuwarden 24 D1
Leeuwin, Cape 84 B6
Le Havre 26 D2
Leiden 24 C2
Leipzig 28 E3
Lek, River 24 C3
Le Mans 26 D2
Lena, River 38 R2
Leningrad 38 G2
Lens 26 F1
Leon (Mexico) 73 B2
Leon (Spain) 30 C2
Lerida 30 F3
Lesotho 61 B3
Lesser Antilles 74 F4
Lewis 20 C1
Lhasa 48 C4
Liberec 36 D3
Liberia 56 B2
Libreville 56 D2
Libya 55 E2
Libyan Desert 55 F2
Liechtenstein 28 D5
Liège 24 D4
Ligurian Sea 33 B3
Likasi 59 B4
Lille 26 F1
Lillehammer 22 B3
Lilongwe 61 C2
Lima 79 C4
Limassol 42 J2
Limoges 26 E4
Limpopo, River 61 B3
Linares 30 D4
Line Islands 83 P9
Linz 28 F4
Lions, Gulf of 26 G5
Lipari Islands 33 E5
Lisbon 30 A4
Lithuania 19 M3
Liverpool 20 E4
Livingstone 61 B2
Ljubljana 35 A1
Llanos 76 C2
Lobito 61 A2
Lodz 36 F3
Lofer 28 E5
Lofoten Islands 22 C2
Logan, Mount 65 E3
Loire, River 26 E3
Lome 56 C2
London (Canada) 65 K5
London (U.K.) 20 G5
Londonderry 20 C3
Lorient 26 C3
Lorraine 26 H2
Los Angeles 71 B3
Louisiana 69 B3
Louisville 69 C3
Lourdes 26 E6
Lower California 73 A2
Lower Hutt 86 E5
Lualaba, River 59 B3
Luanda 61 A1
Lubango 61 A2
Lübeck 28 D2
Lublin 36 H3
Lubumbashi 59 B4
Lucknow 44 D2
Lugano 33 B1
Lule, River 22 E2
Lulea 22 E2
Lusaka 61 B2
Luton 20 F5
Luxembourg 24 E5
Luzern 33 B1
Luzon 46 D2
Lyons 26 G4

Maas, River 24 D3
Maastricht 24 D4
Macao 48 E4
Macdonnell Ranges 84 F4
Machu Picchu 79 C4
Mackenzie River 65 F3

Macquarie Island 88 G
Madagascar 61 D3
Madeira 55 B1
Madeira, River 79 C2
Madras 44 D3
Madrid 30 C3
Madurai 44 C4
Magadan 38 T2
Magdalena, River 79 C2
Magdeburg 28 E2
Magellan's Strait 81 C5
Mahajanga 61 D2
Maiduguri 56 D1
Maine 69 E2
Main, River 28 D3
Majorca 30 G4
Makasar Strait 46 C4
Makgadikgadi Salt Pan 61 B3
Malacca, Straits of 46 B3
Malaga 30 C5
Malawi 61 C2
Malawi, Lake 61 C2
Malay peninsula 40 P8
Malaysia 46 B3
Maldives 44 C4
Mali 55 C3
Malmo 22 C4
Malta 33 E6
Manaar, Gulf of 44 C4
Manado 46 D3
Managua 73 D3
Manapouri, Lake 86 B7
Manaus 79 E2
Manchester 20 E4
Manchuria 48 F2
Mandalay 46 A1
Manila 46 C2
Manitoba 65 J4
Man, Isle of 20 D3
Mannheim 28 C4
Maps 16-17
Maputo 61 C3
Maracaibo 79 C2
Margarita 74 F4
Mariana Trench 82 H7
Maria van Diemen, Cape 86 C2
Market 25, 27, 47, 54, 56, 62
Markham, Mount 88 G
Marquesas Islands 83 R9
Marrakesh 55 B1
Marseilles 26 G5
Marshall Islands 82 L7
Martinique 74 F4
Maryland 69 D2
Maseru 61 B3
Mashhad 42 E2
Massachusetts 69 D2
Massif Central 26 F4
Matadi 59 A3
Mato Grosso plateau 79 E4
Matsuyama 51 B4
Maui 66 G1
Mauna Kea 66 G2
Mauna Loa 66 G2
Mauritania 55 B3
Mauritius 9 S4
Mbabane 61 C3
Mbandaka 59 A2
Mbeya 59 C3
Mbini 56 D2
Mbuji-Mayi 59 B3
McKinley, Mount 66 C2
Mecca 42 D3
Medan 46 A3
Medicine Hat 65 G5
Medina 42 D3
Mediterranean Sea 18 K7
Mekong, River 46 B2
Melanesia 82 J9
Melbourne 84 J7
Melilla 30 D6
Melville Island (Canada) 65 G2
Melville Islands (Australia) 84 E2

Memphis 69 C3
Mendoza 81 C3
Mentawai Islands 46 A4
Meseta 30 C4
Mesopotamia 42 D2
Messina (Italy) 33 E5
Messina (South Africa) 61 C3
Metz 26 H2
Meuse, River 24 D4
Mexico 73 B2
Mexico City 73 B3
Mexico, Gulf of 73 D2
Miami 69 D4
Michigan 69 C2
Michigan, Lake 69 C2
Micronesia 82 K8
Middlesbrough 20 F3
Midway Island 82 L6
Milan 33 B2
Milwaukee 69 B2
Mindanao 46 D3
Minho, River 30 A2
Minneapolis 69 B2
Minnesota 69 B2
Minorca 30 G4
Minsk 38 F3
Miskolc 36 G4
Mississippi River 69 B3
Mississippi State 69 C3
Missouri River 69 B2
Missouri State 69 B2
Mitchell, Mount 69 C3
Mjosa Lake 22 B3
Mobutu Sese Seko, Lake 59 B2
Mogadishu 59 D2
Moldavia 19 N5
Molokai 66 F1
Molucca Sea 46 D4
Mombasa 59 D3
Monaco 26 H5
Mongolia 48 D2
Mongu 61 B2
Monrovia 56 A2
Mons 24 B4
Monsoon 45
Montana 71 B2
Montbéliard 26 H3
Montego Bay 74 C3
Monterrey 73 B2
Montevideo 81 D3
Montgomery 69 C3
Montpellier 26 F6
Montreal 65 L5
Montserrat 74 F3
Moon 4
Moorea 83 Q10
Morava, River 35 C2
Morena, Sierra 30 C4
Morocco 55 C1
Moscow 38 G3
Moselle, River 26 H2
Moshi 59 C3
Mosul 42 D2
Moulmein 46 A2
Mount Isa 84 G4
Mount Newman 84 D4
Mount Pilatus 33 B1
Mozambique 61 C2
Mozambique Channel 61 D2
Mulhacen 30 D5
Mulhouse 26 H3
Mull 20 C2
Multan 44 C1
Munich 28 D4
Münster 28 B3
Muonio, River 22 E2
Murcia 30 E5
Murray, River 84 H6
Murrumbidgee, River 84 J6
Musala 35 C2
Muscat 42 E3
Musgrave Ranges 84 F5
Mutare 61 C2
Mwanza 59 C3
Mweru, Lake 59 B3

Nafud Desert 42 D3
Nagasaki 51 A4
Nagoya 51 C3
Nagpur 44 D2
Nairobi 59 C3
Namib Desert 61 A3
Namibia 61 A3
Namur 24 C4
Nanching 48 E4
Nandi 59 C2
Nanking 48 E3
Nan Shan Mountains 48 C3
Nantes 26 D3
Nao, Cabo de la 30 F4
Napier 86 F4
Naples 33 D4
Nara 51 C4
Narmada, River 44 C2
Narvik 22 D2
Nashville 69 C3
Nassau 74 C1
Nasser, Lake 55 G2
Nauru 82 K9
Nazare 30 A4
Nazareth 42 M2
Ndjamena 55 E3
Ndola 61 B2
Nebraska 71 C2
Negro, River 79 D3
Neisse, River 36 D3
Nelson 86 D5
Nelson, River 65 J4
Nemuro Strait 51 E2
Nepal 44 D2
Netherlands 24 E2
Nevada 71 B3
Nevada, Sierra 30 D5
New Brunswick 65 M5
New Caledonia 82 K11
New Castile 30 D4
Newcastle (Australia) 84 K6
Newcastle (U.K.) 20 E3
Newfoundland 65 N5
New Guinea 82 H9
New Hampshire 69 D2
New Jersey 69 D2
New Mexico 71 C3
New Orleans 69 C4
New Plymouth 86 E4
New Siberian Islands 38 U1
New South Wales 84 J6
New York 69 D2
New York State 69 D2
New Zealand 86
Ngorongoro 59 C3
Niagara Falls 65 L5
Niamey 56 C1
Nicaragua 73 D3
Nice 26 H5
Nicobar Islands 46 A3
Nicosia 42 J1
Niger 55 D3
Niger, River 56 C1
Nigeria 56 C2
Niigata 51 C3
Nijmegen 24 D3
Nile, River 55 G2
Nîmes 26 G5
Nis 35 C2
Nome 66 B2
Norfolk 69 D3
Normandy 26 E5
Norrkoping 22 D4
North America 62
Northampton 20 F4
North Cape 22 E1
North Carolina 69 C3
North Dakota 71 C2
Northern Ireland 20 C3
Northern Territory 84 F3
North European plain 18 L4
North Island, New Zealand 86 D4
North Korea 48 F3

Nafud Desert 42 D3
North Magnetic Pole 89 L
North Pole 89
North Sea 18 H3
North West Highlands 20 D2
North West Territories 65 H3
Norway 22 C3
Norwich 20 G4
Nottingham 20 F4
Nouakchott 55 B3
Nova Scotia 65 M5
Novaya Zemlya 38 J1
Novosibirsk 38 N3
Nullarbor Plain 84 E6
Nuremberg 28 D4

Oahua 66 F1
Oamaru 86 C7
Oban 20 D2
Ob, River 38 K2
Oceans 6-7, 82
Odense 22 C4
Oder, River 36 D2
Odessa 38 F4
Ogbomosho 56 C2
Ogooue, River 56 D3
Ohio 69 C2
Ohio River 69 C3
Ohre, River 36 C3
Oil 43
Okavango Swamp 61 B2
Okayama 51 B4
Okhotsk, Sea of 38 T3
Oki Islands 51 B3
Oklahoma 71 D3
Oklahoma City 71 D3
Oland 22 D4
Old Castile 30 D3
Oldenburg 28 B2
Olomouc 36 E4
Olsztyn 36 G2
Omaha 69 B2
Oman 42 E3
Oman, Gulf of 42 E3
Omdurman 55 F3
Omsk 38 L3
Ontario 65 L5
Ontario, Lake 69 D2
Oporto 30 A3
Oran 55 D1
Orange 26 G4
Orange River 61 A3
Orebro 22 C4
Oregon 71 A2
Ore Mountains 28 E3
Orense 30 B2
Orinoco, River 79 D2
Orkney Islands 20 E1
Orléns 26 E3
Osaka 51 C4
Oslo 22 B4
Ostend 24 A3
Ostersund 22 D3
Ostrava 36 F4
Otaru 51 D2
Otranto, Strait of 33 G4
Ottawa 65 L5
Ouagadougou 56 B1
Oulu 22 F2
Oulu, Lake 22 F3
Oviedo 30 B2
Oxford 20 F5

Pacific Ocean 82 L7
Padang 46 B4
Padua 33 C2
Pakistan 44 B2
Palawan 46 C2
Palembang 46 B4
Palermo 33 D5
Palma 30 G4
Palm Beach 69 D4
Palmerston North 86 E5
Pampas 81 C3
Pamplona 30 E2

Panama 73 E4
Panama Canal 73 D3
Pantellaria 33 D6
Paotow 48 D2
Papua New Guinea 82 H9
Paraguay 81 D2
Paramaribo 79 E2
Parana River 81 D2
Paris 26 F2
Parma 33 C2
Patagonia 81 C4
Patrai 35 C3
Peace River 65 G4
Pecs 36 F5
Pegasus Bay 86 D6
Peking 48 E2
Pemba 59 D3
Pennines 20 E3
Pennsylvania 69 D2
Penzance 20 D5
Perpignan 26 F6
Perth (Australia) 84 B6
Perth (U.K.) 20 E2
Peru 79 C4
Perugia 33 D2
Pescara 33 D3
Philadelphia 69 D3
Philippines 46 C2
Phnom Penh 46 B2
Phoenix 71 B3
Phoenix Islands 82 M9
Picardy 26 F2
Pindus Mountains 35 C3
Pisa 33 C2
Pitcairn Island 83 R11
Pittsburgh 69 C2
Plains 6, 18, 39, 71
Plata, Rio de la 81 D3
Plateau 49, 60
Plates 5
Plenty, Bay of 86 F3
Ploesti 35 D2
Plovdiv 35 D2
Plymouth 20 E5
Plzen 36 C4
Pointe-Noire 59 A3
Poitiers 26 E3
Poland 36 F2
Polar lands 12-13, 88-9
Polar Plateau 88 C
Polynesia 83 N8
Pontianak 46 C4
Poopo, Lake 79 D4
Po, River 33 C2
Port-au-Prince 74 D3
Port Elizabeth 61 B4
Port Harcourt 56 C2
Portland 71 A2
Porto Alegre 79 F5
Port of Spain 74 F4
Port Pirie 84 G6
Port Said 55 G1
Portsmouth 20 F5
Port Sudan 55 G3
Port Talbot 20 D5
Portugal 30 B4
Potsdam 28 E2
Poznań 36 E2
Prague 36 C3
Pretoria 61 B3
Prince Edward Island 65 M5
Prince Edward Islands 9 P5
Prince George 65 G4
Prince Rupert 65 F4
Provence 26 G5
Providence 69 D2
Prudhoe Bay 66 C2
Prut, River 35 D1
Puebla 73 C3
Pueblo 71 C3
Puerto Rico 74 E3
Pune 44 C3
Punta Arenas 81 B5
Pusan 48 G3
Pyongyang 48 F3
Pyrenees 30 F2

94

Qatar 42 E3
Quebec 65 L5
Queen Charlotte Islands 65 E4
Queen Elizabeth Islands 65 J2
Queen Maud Land 88 B
Queensland 84 H4
Queenstown 86 B7
Quetta 44 B1
Quezon City 46 D2
Quito 79 C3
Quiz 90-1

Rabat 55 C1
Radom 36 G3
Railways 29, 39, 50, 64, 85
Rainfall 13, 15, 45
Rangoon 46 A2
Ravenna 33 D2
Rawalpindi 44 C1
Reading 20 F5
Recife 79 G3
Red, River (U.S.A.) 69 B3
Red, River (Vietnam) 46 B1
Red Sea 42 C3
Regensburg 28 D4
Reggio 33 E5
Regina 65 H4
Reims 26 F2
Reindeer Lake 65 H4
Religion 42-3, 45, 46
Rennes 26 D2
Reno 71 B2
Reunion 9 R4
Revilla Gigedo Islands 73 T7
Reykjavik 22 H2
Rhine, River 28 B3
Rhode Island 69 D2
Rhodes 35 D3
Rhodope 35 C2
Rhône, River 26 G4
Rice 45, 47
Richmond 69 D3
Rimini 33 D2
Rio de Janeiro 79 F5
Rio Grande, River 71 C3
Riviera 33 B2
Riyadh 42 D3
Rockhampton 84 J4
Rocky Mountains 62 H4
Romania 35 C1
Rome 33 D4
Rosa, Monte 33 B2
Rosario 81 C3
Ross Ice Shelf 88 H
Ross Sea 88 H
Rostock 28 E1
Rostov 38 H4
Rotorua 86 F4
Rotterdam 24 C3
Rouen 26 E2
Rub 'al Khali 42 D4
Rügen 28 F1
Ruhr, River 28 B3
Ruse 35 D2
Rwanda 59 C3
Ryukyu Islands 40 R6

Saarbrücken 28 B4
Sabah 46 C3
Sable, Cape (Canada) 65 M5
Sable, Cape (U.S.A.) 69 C4
Sacramento 71 B3
Sado 51 C3
Sahara 55 D2
Sahel 52 C4
Sainiaa, Lake 22 F3

Saint Christopher-Nevis 74 F3
Seville 30 C5
Saint Étienne 26 G4
Saint Gallen 33 B1
Saint George's Channel 20 C5
Saint Gotthard tunnel 33 B1
Saint Helena 9 M4
Saint John 65 M5
Saint John's 65 N5
Saint Lawrence River 65 N5
Saint Louis 69 B3
Saint Lucia 74 F4
Saint Malo 26 C2
Saint Nazaire 26 C3
Saint Paul 69 B2
Saint Pierre and Miquelon 65 N5
Saint Vincent and the Grenadines 74 F4
Saint Vincent, Cape 30 A5
Sakai 51 C4
Sakhalin 38 T3
Salamanca 30 C3
Salerno 33 E4
Salt Lake City 71 B2
Salvador 79 G4
Salween, River 46 A2
Salzburg 28 E5
San'a 42 D4
San Antonio 69 B4
San Diego 71 B3
San Francisco 71 B3
San Jose (Costa Rica) 73 D3
San Jose (U.S.A.) 71 A3
San Juan 74 E3
San Lucas, Cape 73 A2
San Marino 33 C3
San Salvador 73 C3
San Sebastian 30 E2
Santa Fe 81 D3
Santander 30 C2
Santarem 30 A4
Santiago (Chile) 81 B3
Santiago (Dominican Republic) 74 D3
Santiago de Cuba 74 C3
Santo Domingo 74 E3
Sao Francisco, River 79 F4
Saône, River 26 G3
Sao Paulo 79 F5
Sao Tome & Principe 56 C2
Sapporo 51 D2
Sarajevo 35 B2
Sarawak 46 C3
Sardinia 33 B4
Sarh 55 E4
Saskatchewan 65 H4
Saskatoon 65 H4
Sassari 33 B4
Saudi Arabia 42 D3
Sault Sainte Marie 65 K5
Savanna 14, 58-9, 79
Sayan Mountains 38 N3
Scale 17
Scandinavia 18 K2
Schelde, River 24 C3
Schwerin 28 D2
Scilly, Isles of 20 C6
Scotland 20 D2
Seasons 13
Seattle 71 A2
Segura, River 30 E4
Seine, River 26 F2
Selvas 76 D3
Semarang 46 B4
Sendai 51 D3
Senegal 56 A1
Senegal, River 55 B3
Seoul 48 F3
Severnaya Zemlya 89 D

Severn, River 20 E4
Seychelles 9 R4
Sfax 55 E1
Shanghai 48 F3
Shannon, River 20 B4
Sheffield 20 F4
Shenyang 48 F2
Shetland Islands 20 G1
Shibeli, River 59 D2
Shikoku 51 B4
Shiraz 42 E3
Sian 48 D3
Siberia 38 N2
Sicily 33 D6
Sidra, Gulf of 55 E1
Siena 33 C3
Sierra Leone 56 A2
Sierra Madre 73 B2
Sierra Nevada 71 B3
Sikhote Alin Range 38 S4
Si Kiang, River 48 D4
Silesia 36 E3
Sinai 55 G3
Singapore 46 B3
Sioux Falls 69 B2
Siracusa 33 E6
Sjaelland 22 C4
Skagen 22 C4
Skagerrak 22 B4
Skopje 35 C2
Skovorodino 38 R3
Skye 22 C2
Snake River 71 B2
Snowdon 20 E4
Society Islands 83 P10
Socotra 42 E4
Sofia 35 C2
Sogne Fjord 22 B3
Solar System 4
Solomon Islands 82 K9
Somali Republic 59 D2
Somerset Islands 65 J2
Sorano 33 C3
Sorfjord 22 B4
South Africa 61 B3
South America 76
Southampton 20 F5
Southampton Island 65 K3
South Australia 84 F5
South Carolina 69 C3
South China Sea 46 C2
South Dakota 71 C2
Southern Alps 86 C6
Southern Uplands 20 E3
South Georgia 88 M
South Island, New Zealand 86 B6
South Korea 48 F3
South Magnetic Pole 88 F
South Orkney Islands 88 M
South Pole 88
South Sandwich Islands 88 M
South Shetland Islands 88 M
Spain 30 C3
Spenser Mountains 86 D6
Spiez 33 A1
Split 35 B2
Spokane 71 B2
Sri Lanka 44 D4
Srinagar 44 C1
Stanley 81 D5
Stanovoy Range 38 R3
Stavanger 22 B4
Steel-works 21
Steppe 38 J3
Stewart Island 86 B8
Stockholm 22 D4
Stoke-on-Trent 20 E4
Storsjon 22 C3
Strasbourg 26 H2
Stuttgart 28 C4
Sucre 79 D4

Sudan 55 G3
Sudbury 65 L5
Suez 55 G2
Suez Canal 55 G1
Sulawesi 46 D4
Sulu Islands 46 D3
Sulu Sea 46 D3
Sumatra 46 B4
Sumbawa 46 C4
Sun 4-5
Sunda Islands 46 C4
Sunderland 20 F3
Sundsvall 22 D3
Sungari, River 48 G2
Superior, Lake 69 C2
Surabaya 46 C4
Surat 44 C2
Surinam 79 E2
Surtsey 22 H2
Svalbard 89 H
Sverdlovsk 38 K3
Sverdrup Islands 65 H2
Swansea 20 E5
Swaziland 61 C3
Sweden 22 D3
Switzerland 33 B1
Sydney 84 K6
Syria 42 C2
Syrian Desert 42 C2
Szczecin 36 D2
Szeged 36 F5

Tabora 59 C3
Tabriz 42 D2
Taegu 48 F3
Tagus, River 30 A4
Tahiti 83 P10
Tainaron, Cape 35 C3
Taipei 48 F4
Taiwan 48 F4
Taiyuan 48 E3
Ta'izz 42 D4
Takla Makan Mountains 48 B3
Tampa 69 C4
Tampere 22 E3
Tana, Lake 59 C1
Tanami Desert 84 F3
Tana, River (Kenya) 59 D3
Tana, River (Norway) 22 F2
Tanega Island 51 B4
Tanga 59 C3
Tanganyika, Lake 59 C3
Tangier 55 C1
Tangshan 48 E3
Tanzania 59 C3
Tapajos, River 79 E3
Taranto 33 F4
Tarim, River 48 B2
Tarragona 30 F3
Tashkent 38 K4
Tasman Bay 86 D5
Tasmania 84 H8
Tatra 36 G4
Taupo, Lake 86 E4
Taurus Mountains 42 C2
Taymyr Peninsula 38 P1
Tbilisi 38 H4
Tea 44, 58
Te Anau, Lake 86 B7
Tegucigalpa 73 D3
Tehran 42 D2
Tel Aviv-Jaffa 42 L2
Telc 36 D4
Tema 56 C2
Temperate lands 12-3
Tennessee 69 C3
Tennessee River 69 C3
Terni 33 D3
Texas 71 D3
Thabana Ntlenyana 61 C3
Thailand 46 B2
Thailand, Gulf of 46 B2
Thames, River 20 F5
Thar 44 C2
The Gulf 42 E3

The Hague 24 C2
Thessaloniki 35 C2
The Wash 20 G4
Thimphu 44 D2
Thionville 26 G2
Thule 89 K
Thunder Bay 65 J5
Tian Shan Mountains 48 B2
Tiber, River 33 D3
Tibesti 55 E2
Tibet 48 B3
Tientsin 48 E3
Tierra del Fuego 81 B5
Tigris, River 42 D2
Tijuana 73 A1
Tilburg 24 D3
Timaru 86 C7
Timbuktu 55 C3
Timisoara 35 C1
Timor 46 D4
Timor Sea 84 B2
Tirane 35 B2
Tisza, River 36 G5
Titicaca, Lake 79 D4
Togo 56 C2
Tokelau Islands 82 M9
Tokyo 51 C3
Toledo (Spain) 30 D4
Toledo (U.S.A.) 69 C2
Toliara 61 D3
Tone, River 51 C3
Tonga 82 M11
Tonle Sap 46 B2
Toowoomba 84 K5
Torne, River 22 E2
Toronto 65 K5
Torrens, Lake 84 G6
Torreon 73 B2
Torres Strait 84 H1
Torun 36 F2
Toubkal 55 C1
Toulon 26 G5
Toulouse 26 E6
Tourism 31, 32, 34, 59, 75
Tours 26 E3
Townsville 84 J3
Toyama 51 C3
Trains 29, 39, 50, 64, 85
Transylvanian Alps 35 C1
Trent, River 20 F4
Trieste 33 D2
Trinidad & Tobago 74 G4
Tripoli 55 E1
Tristan da Cunha 9 M5
Tromso 22 E2
Trondheim 22 C3
Troyes 26 F2
Trujillo 79 C3
Tsangpo, River 48 B4
Tsinan 48 E3
Tsingtao 48 F3
Tsitsihar 48 F2
Tsugaru, Strait 51 D2
Tsushima 51 B4
Tuamotu Archipelago 83 R10
Tubuai Islands 83 P11
Tucson 71 C3
Tucuman 81 C2
Tulsa 69 B3
Tunis 55 E1
Tunisia 55 D1
Turin 33 B2
Turkana, Lake 59 C2
Turkey 42 C2
Turks Islands 74 D2
Turku 22 E3
Tuvalu 82 L9
Tyrol 33 C1
Tyrrhenian Sea 33 D5

Ubangi, River 59 A2
Udine 33 D1
Uganda 59 C2
Ujung Pandang 46 C4
Ukraine 19 N5

Ulan Bator 48 D2
Ulan Ude 38 P3
Ume, River 22 D3
Union of Soviet Socialist Republics 38
United Arab Emirates 42 E3
United Kingdom 20 G4
United Nations 8
United States of America 66
Uppsala 22 D4
Ural Mountains 38 J3
Ural, River 38 J4
Urmia, Lake 42 D2
Urumchi 48 B2
U.S.A. 66
Ushant 26 B2
U.S.S.R. 38
Utah 71 B3
Utrecht 24 D2
Utsunomiya 51 C3

Vaal, River 61 B3
Vaasa 22 E3
Valence 26 G4
Valencia 30 E4
Valenciennes 26 F1
Valladolid 30 C3
Valletta 33 E6
Valparaiso 81 B3
Vancouver 65 G4
Vancouver Island 65 F5
Vaner, Lake 22 C4
Van, Lake 42 D2
Vanuatu 82 K10
Varanasi 44 D3
Vardo 22 G1
Varna 35 D2
Vasteras 22 D4
Vatican City 33 C4
Vatnajokull 22 J2
Vatter, Lake 22 C4
Venezuela 79 D2
Venice 33 D2
Verkhoyansk Range 38 R2
Vermont 69 D2
Verona 33 C2
Vesteralen 22 D2
Vesuvius 33 E4
Victoria (Australia) 84 H7
Victoria (Canada) 65 F5
Victoria Falls 61 B2
Victoria Island 65 H2
Victoria, Lake 59 C3
Victoria Land 88 G
Vienna 28 F4
Vientiane 46 B2
Vietnam 46 C2
Vigo 30 A2
Virginia 69 D3
Virgin Islands 74 F3
Viscount Melville Sound 65 H2
Vishakhapatnam 44 D3
Vistula, River 36 F2
Vitoria 30 D2
Volos 35 C3
Volta, Lake 56 B2
Vosges 26 H2
Vostok 88 E

Waal, River 24 D3
Wadden Zee 24 D1
Wadi Halfa 55 G2
Waikato, River 86 E4
Waitaki, River 86 C7
Wake Island 82 K7
Wakkanai 51 D1

Walcheren Island 24 B3
Wales 20 E4
Walvis Bay 61 A3
Wanaka, Lake 86 B7
Wanganui 86 E4
Warrego, River 84 J5
Warsaw 36 G2
Warta, River 36 E2
Wasatch Range 71 B3
Washington 69 D3
Washington State 71 A2
Waterfall 61, 64
Waterford 20 C4
Weddell Sea 88 M
Weipa 84 H2
Wellington 86 E5
Weser, River 28 C2
West Bank 42 M2
Western Australia 84 D5
Western Ghats 44 C3
Western Sahara 55 B2
Western Samoa 82 M10
West Indies 74
Westland Bight 86 B6
West Virginia 69 C3
Wexford 20 C4
Whangarei 86 E2
White Nile 55 G3
White Sea 18 Q1
Whitney, Mount 71 B3
Whyalla 84 G6
Wichita 69 B3
Wick 20 E1
Wicklow Mountains 20 C4
Wiesbaden 28 C3
Wight, Isle of 20 F5
Wilkes Land 88 F
Windhoek 61 A3
Windward Passage 74 D3
Winnipeg 65 H5
Winnipeg, Lake 65 J4
Winterthur 33 B1
Wisconsin 69 C2
Wollongong 84 K6
Worcester 20 E4
Wrangel Island 38 W1
Wroclaw 36 E3
Wuhan 48 E3
Würzburg 28 D4
Wye, River 20 E4
Wyndham 84 E3
Wyoming 71 C2

Yakutsk 38 R2
Yangtze, River 48 E3
Yaounde 56 D2
Yellowknife 65 G3
Yellow Sea 48 F3
Yellowstone, River 71 C2
Yemen 42 D4
Yenisey, River 38 M2
Yokohama 51 C3
York 20 F4
York, Cape 84 H2
Yucatan 73 D3
Yugoslavia 35 B2
Yukon, River 66 C2
Yukon Territory 65 E3

Zagreb 35 B1
Zagros Mountains 42 D2
Zaire 59 B3
Zaire, River 59 B2
Zambezi River 61 C2
Zambia 61 B2
Zamboanga 46 D3
Zanzibar 59 D3
Zaragoza 30 E3
Zaria 56 C1
Zeebrugge 24 A3
Zimbabwe 61 B2
Zürich 33 B1
Zwolle 24 E2

95

ANSWERS TO QUESTIONS

Answers to text questions

page 18 Western Europe's most important building: the Headquarters of the European Community in Brussels, the capital of Belgium. In this building many of the important decisions about Western Europe are made. The photograph shows reflections in the double-glazed windows. In the reflection you can see small old houses and shops and big modern office buildings in Brussels, the biggest city in Belgium.

page 19 B = Belgium; D = Germany (Deutschland in German); DK = Denmark; E = Spain (España); F = France; GB = Great Britain; GR = Greece; I = Italy; IRL = Ireland (Republic of Ireland); L = Luxembourg; NL = Netherlands; P = Portugal.

page 21 The London landmarks featured on the stamp are (*left to right*): Westminster Abbey; Nelson's column (in Trafalgar Square); statue of Eros in Piccadilly Circus; Telecom Tower; clock tower of the Houses of Parliament (containing the bell Big Ben); St Paul's Cathedral; Tower Bridge; White Tower of the Tower of London.

page 25 Belgium has two official languages, French and Flemish. The coin on the left has the French name for Belgium, that on the right its Flemish name.

page 27 The vegetables on the stall are green and red peppers, aubergines, onions and tomatoes, with some cucumbers and baby marrows on the left.

page 29 The international clock in Berlin: the names on the clock stay still; the numbers move slowly round. In 24 hours, the numbers have turned a full circle – just like the Earth in space! When the photograph was taken, at 16.00 hours (4 pm) in Berlin, it was 13.30 hours (1.30 pm) in Reykjavik, Iceland, and 17.00 hours (5 pm) in Helsinki, Finland. In places *west* of Berlin it is earlier in the day; in places *east* of Berlin, it is later in the day. Note the names on the clock are in German.

page 55 Puzzle picture: the circles are 'drawn' by huge centre-pivot irrigation sprays, which turn slowly to make the shape of a circle. Each circle is about 1 kilometre across. The irrigation allows crops to grow in the desert. Some of the crops in the circular 'fields' are already ripening, so they look less green.

page 57 Puzzle picture: this farmer in Ghana is making a mound of earth over each yam tuber he has planted.

page 62 The photograph of the fruit market shows (*at back*) bananas, pineapple; (*centre*) breadfruit, mango, lime; (*at front*) grapefruit, lemons, pawpaw, pineapple. There are vegetables on display behind.

page 63 The north shores of Lakes Superior, Huron, Erie and Ontario are in Canada, and the south shores in the USA. Lake Michigan is entirely in the USA.

page 63 El Salvador only has a coastline on the Pacific Ocean. Belize only has a coastline on the Caribbean Sea. (Honduras has a tiny coastline on the Pacific – look closely at the map!)

page 67 Seattle to Miami is 5445 kilometres; New Orleans to Chicago is 1488 kilometres.

page 69 The stamp shows the Mississippi river. It flows southwards to New Orleans and the Gulf of Mexico. It was used for transport far into the heart of America long before roads were built, so it became known as the 'Great River Road'.

Answers to quiz

Name the island
(Name of country in brackets after name of island)
1 Iceland (Iceland); 2 Crete (Greece); 3 Sicily (Italy); 4 Sumatra (Indonesia); 5 Sulawesi (Indonesia); 6 Cuba (Cuba); 7 Honshu (Japan); 8 Baffin Island (Canada); 9 Madagascar (Madagascar); 10 North Island (New Zealand)

Name the country
(Name of continent in brackets after name of country)
1 Norway (Europe); 2 Thailand (Asia); 3 Mozambique (Africa); 4 Mexico (Central America); 5 Chile (South America).

Oceans and seas
1 Pacific; 2 Atlantic; 3 Arctic; 4 Indian; 5 Atlantic; 6 Red Sea; 7 Sea of Japan; 8 North Sea; 9 South China Sea; 10 Caribbean Sea.

A mystery message
I was *hungry*, so I bought a large *turkey*, some *swedes* and a bottle of *port*. Finally, I ate an *ice*-cream. I enjoyed my *meal*, but afterwards I began to *bulge* and I got a bad *pain*. A *man* told me: 'Just eat *pineapples* and *egg* cooked in a *pan*. Tomorrow you can eat a *banana* and some *Brazil* nuts. It shouldn't *cost* you too much.' I said: 'You must be *mad*! I think I've got *malaria*. I'll have *to go* to a doctor quickly, otherwise I'll soon be *dead*.'
Happily, the doctor *cured* me, so I am still *alive* today!

Places in Asia
Countries Iran; China; Oman; Taiwan.
Capital cities Manila; Delhi; Kabul; Peking; Seoul; Riyadh.

Colour quiz
1 Red (Red Sea/Red River); 2 Green (Greenland/Green Bay); 3 Black (Black Sea/Black Forest); 4 Yellow (Yellow Sea/Yellowstone River); 5 White (White Sea/White Nile); 6 Orange (Orange/Orange River); 7 Blue (Blue Nile/Blue Ridge, USA).

Score
13–14 Brilliant! 10–12 Very well done. 6–9 Good. 2–5 Use this atlas more – you'll soon do better. 0–1 Try another planet – there's less geography there.

States of the USA
1 Texas; 2 Rhode Island; 3 Minnesota; 4 Florida; 5 California; 6 Maine; 7 Michigan; 8 Maryland; 9 Wyoming and Colorado; 10 Oklahoma; 11 Michigan; 12 New York; 13 Utah; 14 Louisiana; 15 South Dakota; 16 North Carolina; 17 Utah, Colorado, Arizona and New Mexico; 18 Four; 19 Three; 20 Five.

Great rivers of Europe
1 Danube; 2 Rhine; 3 Rhône; 4 Severn; 5 Tagus.

Illustration Acknowledgements
The Australian Tourist Commission p. 85 (top); *Bruce Coleman Limited* p. 6, p. 8, p. 11 (right), p. 15 (left), p. 21 (below right), p. 23 (above right), p. 27 (top), p. 29 (below left), p. 32 (below), p. 37 (top), p. 39 (below), p. 40, p. 54 (top), p. 59, p. 61 (right), p. 69 (above left), p. 70 (top left and below), p. 72 (top), p. 78 (top), p. 80 (below), p. 82, p. 83, p. 87, p. 89 (below); *The Daily Telegraph* p. 5; *Susan Griggs* p. 11 (left), p. 21 (top), p. 23 (below right), p. 31 (top), p. 33, p. 38, p. 39 (top), p. 42 (right), p. 43 (top), p. 45 (below), p. 50 (above left), p. 62, p. 63, p. 65 (right), p. 67, p. 70 (top right), p. 72 (below), p. 73, p. 76; *Robert Harding Picture Library* p. 15 (right), p. 19, p. 41, p. 45 (centre), p. 47 (top), p. 49 (centre and below left), p. 50 (below), p. 58 (below left), p. 61 (left), p. 64 (left), p. 75 (top left), p. 78 (below left), p. 88; *The J. Allan Cash Photolibrary* p. 12, p. 25 (below right), p. 29 (right), p. 31 (below right), p. 45 (top), p. 48, p. 50 (above right), p. 54 (below left), p. 56, p. 57 (top left), p. 58 (top and below right), p. 75 (below), p. 78 (below right); *NASA* title page, p. 55 (below left); *The Quentin Bell Organisation* p. 64 (right); *Ralph Somerville* p. 49 (top); *Spanish National Tourist Office* p. 31 (centre); *Vautier-de-Nanxe* p. 42 (left), p. 71, p. 77, p. 80 (top), p. 81; *David and Jill Wright* p. 10, p. 14, p. 16, p. 18, p. 21 (below right), p. 22, p. 23 (below left), p. 25 (top and below left), p. 27 (centre and below), p. 29 (top), p. 31 (below right), p. 34 (left), p. 35, p.43 (below), p. 44, p. 47 (below left), p. 52, p. 54 (below right), p. 57 (top right, centre and below), p. 60, p. 68 (above), p. 69 (centre and top right), p. 75 (top right), p. 85 (centre); *Zefa* p. 11 (centre), p. 20, p. 23 (above left), p. 24, p. 28, p. 32 (top), p. 34 (right), p. 37 (below, right and left), p. 53, p. 55 (below right), p. 65 (left), p. 68 (below), p. 79, p. 89 (centre).